Presented To: _____

From: _____

Date: _____

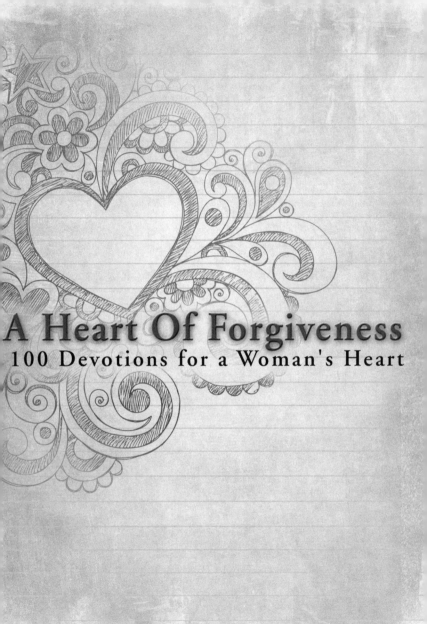

A Heart Of Forgiveness

100 Devotions for a Woman's Heart

The quoted ideas expressed in this book (but not Scripture verses) are not, in all cases, exact quotations, as some have been edited for clarity and brevity. In all cases, the author has attempted to maintain the speaker's original intent. In some cases, quoted material for this book was obtained from secondary sources, primarily print media. While every effort was made to ensure the accuracy of these sources, the accuracy cannot be guaranteed. For additions, deletions, corrections, or clarifications in future editions of this text, please write Freeman-Smith, LLC.

Cover Design by Kim Russell / Wahoo Designs
Page Layout by Bart Dawson

ISBN 978-1-60587-259-9

Printed in the United States of America

A Heart Of Forgiveness
100 Devotions for a Woman's Heart

Introduction

As you make plans for the day ahead, here's a question: whom do you need to forgive today?

If you're like most folks, you probably find it difficult to forgive the people who have harmed you. No matter. As a Christian, you are commanded to forgive others, just as you, too, have been forgiven. So even when forgiveness is difficult, you must ask God to help you move beyond the spiritual stumbling blocks of bitterness, anger, hatred, and regret.

When you forgive those who have hurt you, you honor God by obeying His commandments. But, when you harbor bitterness against others, your disobedience brings suffering—needless suffering—upon you and your loved ones.

In your hands, you hold a book that contains 100 devotional readings. These readings contain Bible verses, brief essays, inspirational quotations from noted Christians, and prayers.

During the next 100 days, please try this experiment: read a page from this book each day. If you're already committed to a daily time of worship, this book will enrich that experience. If you are not, the simple act of giving God a few minutes each morning will change the direction and the quality of your life.

Each day provides opportunities to put God where He belongs: at the center of our lives. When we do so, we worship Him, not just with words, but with deeds. And, we become dutiful servants of the God who shares His Son's message of love and salvation with the world.

May you be such a servant—a woman with a generous spirit and a forgiving heart.

Forgive Everybody

For if you forgive people their wrongdoing, your Heavenly Father will forgive you as well. But if you don't forgive people, your Father will not forgive your wrongdoing.

Matthew 6:14-15 HCSB

The world holds few if any rewards for those who remain angrily focused upon the past. Still, the act of forgiveness is difficult for all but the most saintly men and women. Are you mired in the quicksand of bitterness or regret? If so, you are not only disobeying God's Word, you are also wasting your time.

Being frail, fallible, imperfect human beings, most of us are quick to anger, quick to blame, slow to forgive, and even slower to forget. Yet as Christians, we are commanded to forgive others, just as we, too, have been forgiven.

If there exists even one person—alive or dead—against whom you hold bitter feelings, it's time to forgive. Or, if you are embittered against yourself for some past mistake or shortcoming, it's finally time to forgive yourself and move on. Hatred, bitterness, and regret are not part of God's plan for your life. Forgiveness is.

A Heart of Forgiveness

Forgiveness is its own reward. Bitterness is its own punishment. Guard your words and your thoughts accordingly.

Be even-tempered, content with second place, quick to forgive an offense. Forgive as quickly and completely as the Master forgave you. And regardless of what else you put on, wear love. It's your basic, all-purpose garment. Never be without it.

—

Colossians 3:13-14 MSG

The fact is, God no longer deals with us in judgment but in mercy. If people got what they deserved, this old planet would have ripped apart at the seams centuries ago. Praise God that because of His great love "we are not consumed, for his compassions never fail" (Lam. 3:22).

Joni Eareckson Tada

When God forgives, He forgets. He buries our sins in the sea and puts a sign on the shore saying, "No Fishing Allowed."

Corrie ten Boom

God expects us to forgive others as He has forgiven us; we are to follow His example by having a forgiving heart.

Vonette Bright

Forgiveness is the precondition of love.

Catherine Marshall

Today's Prayer

Dear Lord, let forgiveness rule my heart, even when forgiveness is difficult. Let me be Your obedient servant, Lord, and let me be a woman who forgives others just as You have forgiven me. Amen

Give Him Your Heart

For God so loved the world that He gave His only begotten Son, that whoever believes in Him should not perish but have everlasting life.

John 3:16 NKJV

Your decision to allow Christ to reign over your heart is the pivotal decision of your life. It is a decision that you cannot ignore. It is a decision that is yours and yours alone.

God's love for you is deeper and more profound than you can imagine. God's love for you is so great that He sent His only Son to this earth to die for your sins and to offer you the priceless gift of eternal life. Now, you must decide whether or not to accept God's gift. Will you ignore it or embrace it? Will you return it or neglect it? Will you accept Christ's love and build a lifelong relationship with Him, or will you turn away from Him and take a different path?

Accept God's gift now: allow His Son to preside over your heart, your thoughts, and your life, starting this very instant.

Guard Your Heart

The ultimate choice for you is the choice to invite God's Son into your heart. Choose wisely . . . and immediately.

It's your heart that Jesus longs for: your will to be made His own with self on the cross forever, and Jesus alone on the throne.

Ruth Bell Graham

The amount of power you experience to live a victorious, triumphant Christian life is directly proportional to the freedom you give the Spirit to be Lord of your life!

Anne Graham Lotz

Choose Jesus Christ! Deny yourself, take up the Cross, and follow Him—for the world must be shown. The world must see, in us, a discernible, visible, startling difference.

Elisabeth Elliot

Jesus is the personal approach from the unseen God coming so near that he becomes inescapable. You don't have to find him—you just have to consent to be found.

E. Stanley Jones

Today's Prayer

Dear Lord, You sent Your Son to this earth that we might have the gift of eternal life. Thank You, Father, for that priceless gift. Help me to share the wondrous message of Jesus with others so that they, too, might accept Him as their Savior. And, let me praise You always for the new life You have given me, a life that is both abundant and eternal. Amen

Put God
in His Rightful Place

Do not have other gods besides Me.

Exodus 20:3 HCSB

As you think about the nature of your relationship with God, remember this: you will always have some type of relationship with Him—it is inevitable that your life must be lived in relationship to God. The question is not if you will have a relationship with Him; the burning question is whether that relationship will be one that seeks to honor Him . . . or not.

Are you willing to place God first in your life? And, are you willing to welcome Him into your heart? Unless you can honestly answer these questions with a resounding yes, then your relationship with God isn't what it could be or should be. Thankfully, God is always available, He's always ready to forgive, and He's waiting to hear from you now. The rest, of course, is up to you.

Guard Your Heart

You must guard your heart by putting God in His rightful place—first place.

And I pray this: that your love will keep on growing in knowledge and every kind of discernment, so that you can determine what really matters and can be pure and blameless in the day of Christ.

—

Philippians 1:9 HCSB

If God has the power to create and sustain the universe, He is more than able to sustain your marriage and your ministry, your faith and your finances, your hope and your health.

Anne Graham Lotz

Love has its source in God, for love is the very essence of His being.

Kay Arthur

It is when we come to the Lord in our nothingness, our powerlessness and our helplessness that He then enables us to love in a way which, without Him, would be absolutely impossible.

Elisabeth Elliot

When all else is gone, God is still left. Nothing changes Him.

Hannah Whitall Smith

Today's Prayer

Dear Lord, Your love is eternal and Your laws are everlasting. When I obey Your commandments, I am blessed. Today, I invite You to reign over every corner of my heart. I will have faith in You, Father. I will sense Your presence; I will accept Your love; I will trust Your will; and I will praise You for the Savior of my life: Your Son Jesus. Amen

Listening to God

The one who is from God listens to God's words. This is why you don't listen, because you are not from God.

John 8:47 HCSB

Sometimes God speaks loudly and clearly. More often, He speaks in a quiet voice—and if you are wise, you will be listening carefully when He does. To do so, you must carve out quiet moments each day to study His Word and sense His direction.

Can you quiet yourself long enough to listen to your conscience? Are you attuned to the subtle guidance of your intuition? Are you willing to pray sincerely and then to wait quietly for God's response? Hopefully so. Usually God refrains from sending His messages on stone tablets or city billboards. More often, He communicates in subtler ways. If you sincerely desire to hear His voice, you must listen carefully, and you must do so in the silent corners of your quiet, willing heart.

A Heart of Forgiveness

God is trying to get your attention. And, He wants you to make peace with your past. Are you listening?

When we come to Jesus stripped of pretensions, with a needy spirit, ready to listen, He meets us at the point of need.

Catherine Marshall

In the soul-searching of our lives, we are to stay quiet so we can hear Him say all that He wants to say to us in our hearts.

Charles Swindoll

The center of power is not to be found in summit meetings or in peace conferences. It is not in Peking or Washington or the United Nations, but rather where a child of God prays in the power of the Spirit for God's will to be done in her life, in her home, and in the world around her.

Ruth Bell Graham

We must leave it to God to answer our prayers in His own wisest way. Sometimes, we are so impatient and think that God does not answer. God always answers! He never fails! Be still. Abide in Him.

Mrs. Charles E. Cowman

Today's Prayer

Lord, give me the wisdom to be a good listener. Help me listen carefully to my family, to my friends, and—most importantly— to You. Amen

Praying About Forgiveness

Rejoice in hope; be patient in affliction; be persistent in prayer.

Romans 12:12 HCSB

If forgiveness were easy, everyone would be doing it. If forgiveness were as simple as adding two plus two, we wouldn't be so concerned about it, and neither would God. But God has much to say about forgiveness, and for a very good reason: He knows that forgiveness isn't easy. To the contrary, forgiveness can be very hard work. Thankfully, forgiveness is also very rewarding work for those who are wise enough to heed God's Word.

If forgiveness is difficult for you, don't fret about it, pray about it. The work of forgiveness begins with prayer. Prayer is the most effective way to cleanse your heart of anger and restore your sense of peace.

For whom should you pray? There are two people in particular: first, for the person who has hurt you, and second, for the person in the mirror. Praying for yourself may be easy; praying for the other person may be considerably harder, but that's okay with God. He knows you're up to the task. And now, it's time to get busy doing the hard work of forgiveness. So with no further ado, you may bow your head.

Rejoice evermore. Pray without ceasing. In every thing give thanks: for this is the will of God in Christ Jesus concerning you.

1 Thessalonians 5:16-18 KJV

The intense prayer of the righteous is very powerful.

James 5:16 HCSB

Therefore I say to you, whatever things you ask when you pray, believe that you receive them, and you will have them.

Mark 11:24 NKJV

I sought the LORD, and he heard me, and delivered me from all my fears.

Psalm 34:4 KJV

A Heart of Forgiveness

Prayer changes things and it changes you. So if you genuinely want a more forgiving heart, pray about it.

Repentance removes old sins and wrong attitudes, and it opens the way for the Holy Spirit to restore our spiritual health.

Shirley Dobson

God gives us permission to forget our past and the understanding to live our present. He said He will remember our sins no more. (Psalm 103:11-12)

Serita Ann Jakes

When we reach the end of our strength, wisdom, and personal resources, we enter into the beginning of his glorious provisions.

Patsy Clairmont

In those desperate times when we feel like we don't have an ounce of strength, He will gently pick up our heads so that our eyes can behold something—something that will keep His hope alive in us.

Kathy Troccoli

Today's Prayer

Dear Lord, make me a woman of constant prayer. Your Holy Word commands me to pray without ceasing. In all things great and small, at all times, whether happy or sad, let me seek Your wisdom and Your strength . . . in prayer. Amen

Study His Word

You will be a good servant of Christ Jesus, nourished by the words of the faith and of the good teaching that you have followed.

1 Timothy 4:6 HCSB

God's Word is unlike any other book. The Bible is a roadmap for life here on earth and for life eternal. As Christians, we are called upon to study God's Holy Word, to trust its promises, to follow its commandments, and to share its Good News with the world.

As women who seek to follow in the footsteps of the One from Galilee, we must study the Bible and meditate upon its meaning for our lives. Otherwise, we deprive ourselves of a priceless gift from our Creator. God's Holy Word is, indeed, a transforming, life-changing, one-of-a-kind treasure. And, a passing acquaintance with the Good Book is insufficient for Christians who seek to obey God's Word and to understand His will.

Seeking God's Wisdom

On your bookshelf you have God's roadmap for life here on earth and for life eternal. How you choose to use your Bible is, of course, up to you . . . and so are the consequences.

*For I am not ashamed of the gospel,
because it is God's power for salvation to
everyone who believes.*

—

Romans 1:16 HCSB

Weave the unveiling fabric of God's word through your heart and mind. It will hold strong, even if the rest of life unravels.

Gigi Graham Tchividjian

I need the spiritual revival that comes from spending quiet time alone with Jesus in prayer and in thoughtful meditation on His Word.

Anne Graham Lotz

God can see clearly no matter how dark or foggy the night is. Trust His Word to guide you safely home.

Lisa Whelchel

Words fail to express my love for this holy Book, my gratitude for its author, for His love and goodness. How shall I thank him for it?

Lottie Moon

Today's Prayer

Dear Lord, the Bible is Your gift to me; let me use it. When I stray from Your Holy Word, Lord, I suffer. But, when I place Your Word at the very center of my life, I am blessed. Make me a faithful student of Your Word so that I might be a faithful servant in Your world, this day and every day. Amen

Defeating Procrastination

When you make a vow to God, don't delay fulfilling it, because He does not delight in fools. Fulfill what you vow.

Ecclesiastes 5:4 HCSB

There's never a "perfect" time to do anything. That's why we can always find reasons to put off until tomorrow the things that we should be doing today.

If you find yourself bound by the chains of procrastination, ask yourself what you're waiting for—or more accurately what you're afraid of—and why. As you examine the emotional roadblocks that have, heretofore, blocked your path, you may discover that you're waiting for the "perfect" moment, that instant in time when you feel neither afraid nor anxious. But in truth, perfect moments like these are few and far between.

So stop waiting for the perfect moment and focus, instead, on finding the right moment to do what needs to be done. Then, trust God and get busy. When you do, you'll discover that you and the Father, working together, can accomplish great things . . . and that you can accomplish them sooner rather than later.

Once you acquire the habit of doing what needs to be done when it needs to be done, you will avoid untold trouble, heartache, and stress. So learn to defeat procrastination by paying less attention to your fears and more

25

attention to your responsibilities. God has created a world that punishes procrastinators and rewards men and women who "do it now". In other words, life doesn't procrastinate. Neither should you.

Guard Your Heart

The habit of procrastination is often rooted in the fear of failure, the fear of discomfort, or the fear of embarrassment. Your challenge is to confront these fears and defeat them.

Do the unpleasant work first and enjoy the rest of the day.

Marie T. Freeman

We spend our lives dreaming of the future, not realizing that a little of it slips away every day.

Barbara Johnson

Do noble things, do not dream them all day long.

Charles Kingsley

Today's Prayer

Dear Lord, today is a new day. Help me tackle the important tasks immediately, even if those tasks are unpleasant. Don't let me put off until tomorrow what I should do today. Amen

Making God's Priorities Your Priorities

Draw near to God, and He will draw near to you.

James 4:8 HCSB

Do you invest more time that you should reliving the past? Are you troubled by feelings of anger, envy, bitterness, or regret? Do you harbor ill will against someone whom you simply can't seem to forgive? If so, it's time to finally get serious about forgiveness.

When someone hurts you badly, the act of forgiveness is difficult, but necessary. Until you forgive, you are trapped in a prison of your own creation. But what if you have tried to forgive and simply can't seem to do so? The solution to your dilemma is this: you must make forgiveness a higher priority in your life.

Most of us don't spend too much time thinking about forgiveness; we worry, instead, about the injustices we have suffered and the people who inflicted them. God has a better plan: He wants us to live in the present, not the past, and He knows that in order to do so, we must forgive those who have harmed us.

Have you made forgiveness a high priority? Have you sincerely asked God to forgive you for your inability to forgive others? Have you genuinely prayed that bitterness

27

might be swept from your heart? If so, congratulations. If not, perhaps it's time to rearrange your priorities.

Guard Your Heart

The priorities you choose will dictate the life you live. So choose carefully.

How important it is for us—young and old—to live as if Jesus would return any day—to set our goals, make our choices, raise our children, and conduct business with the perspective of the imminent return of our Lord.

Gloria Gaither

The essence of the Christian life is Jesus: that in all things He might have the preeminence, not that in some things He might have a place.

Franklin Graham

Today's Prayer

Lord, let Your priorities be my priorities. Let Your will be my will. Let Your Word be my guide, and let me grow in faith and in wisdom this day and every day. Amen

Have a Regular Appointment with God

He awakens Me morning by morning, He awakens My ear to hear as the learned. The Lord God has opened My ear.

Isaiah 50:4-5 NKJV

Each new day is a gift from God, and if we are wise, we will spend a few quiet moments each morning thanking the Giver. Daily life is woven together with the threads of habit, and no habit is more important to our spiritual health than the discipline of daily prayer and devotion to the Creator.

When we begin each day with our heads bowed and hearts lifted, we remind ourselves of God's love, His protection, and His commandments. And if we are wise, we align our priorities for the coming day with the teachings that God has given us through His Holy Word.

Are you seeking to change some aspect of your life? Do you seek to improve the condition of your spiritual or physical health? If so, ask for God's help and ask for it many times each day . . . starting with your morning devotional.

Seeking God's Wisdom

You need a regular appointment with your Creator. God is ready to talk to you, and you should prepare yourself each morning to talk to Him.

We are meddling with God's business when we let all manner of imaginings loose, predicting disaster, contemplating possibilities instead of following, one day at a time, God's plain and simple pathway.

Elisabeth Elliot

Jesus challenges you and me to keep our focus daily on the cross of His will if we want to be His disciples.

Anne Graham Lotz

A person with no devotional life generally struggles with faith and obedience.

Charles Stanley

Today's Prayer

Dear Lord, every day of my life is a journey with You. I will take time today to think, to pray, and to study Your Word. Guide my steps, Father, and keep me mindful that today offers yet another opportunity to celebrate Your blessings, Your love, and Your Son. Amen

Making the Choice to Forgive

I have set before you life and death, blessing and curse. Choose life so that you and your descendants may live, love the Lord your God, obey Him, and remain faithful to Him. For He is your life, and He will prolong your life in the land the Lord swore to give to your fathers Abraham, Isaac, and Jacob.

Deuteronomy 30:19-20 HCSB

Forgiveness is a choice. We can either choose to forgive those who have injured us, or not. When we obey God by offering forgiveness to His children, we are blessed. But when we allow bitterness and resentment to poison our hearts, we are tortured by our own shortsightedness.

Do you harbor resentment against anyone? If so, you are faced with an important decision: whether or not to forgive the person who has hurt you. God's instructions are clear: He commands you to forgive. God doesn't suggest that you forgive or request that you forgive; He commands it. Period.

To forgive or not to forgive: that is the question. The answer should be obvious. The time to forgive is now because tomorrow may be too late . . . for you.

A Heart of Forgiveness

Every day you make hundreds of choices . . . and the quality of those choices determines the quality of your day and your life.

Freedom is not the right to do what we want but the power to do what we ought.

Corrie ten Boom

No matter how many books you read, no matter how many schools you attend, you're never really wise until you start making choices that are pleasing to God.

Marie T. Freeman

There may be no trumpet sound or loud applause when we make a right decision, just a calm sense of resolution and peace.

Gloria Gaither

Today's Prayer

Heavenly Father, I have many choices to make. Help me choose wisely as I follow in the footsteps of Your only begotten Son. Amen

The Good News

Grace to you and peace from God our Father and the Lord Jesus Christ.

Philippians 1:2 HCSB

God's grace is not earned . . . thank goodness! To earn God's love and His gift of eternal life would be far beyond the abilities of even the most righteous man or woman. Thankfully, grace is not an earthly reward for righteous behavior; it is a blessed spiritual gift which can be accepted by believers who dedicate themselves to God through Christ. When we accept Christ into our hearts, we are saved by His grace.

The familiar words of Ephesians 2:8 make God's promise perfectly clear: It is by grace we have been saved, through faith. We are saved not because of our good deeds but because of our faith in Christ.

God's grace is the ultimate gift, and we owe to Him the ultimate in thanksgiving. Let us praise the Creator for His priceless gift, and let us share the Good News with all who cross our paths. We return our Father's love by accepting His grace and by sharing His message and His love. When we do, we are eternally blessed . . . and the Father smiles.

A Heart of Forgiveness

By God's grace, you are forgiven. Now, your challenge is to forgive everybody, including yourself.

Forgiveness is God's command.

Martin Luther

I believe that forgiveness can become a continuing cycle: because God forgives us, we're to forgive others; because we forgive others, God forgives us. Scripture presents both parts of the cycle.

Shirley Dobson

When God forgives, He forgets. He buries our sins in the sea and puts a sign on the shore saying, "No Fishing Allowed."

Corrie ten Boom

Today's Prayer

Dear Lord, I have fallen short of Your commandments, and You have forgiven me. You have blessed me with Your love and Your mercy. Enable me to be merciful toward others, Father, just as You have been merciful to me, and let me share Your love with all whom I meet. Amen

Forgiveness Now

Therefore, get your minds ready for action, being self-disciplined . . . .

1 Peter 1:13 HCSB

How often should we forgive other people? More times than we can count. That's a tall order, of course, but we must remember that it's an order from God—an order that must be obeyed.

In God's curriculum, forgiveness isn't optional; it's a required course. Sometimes, of course, we find it very difficult to forgive the people who have hurt us badly. But if we fail to forgive others, we hurt ourselves most of all. When our hearts are filled with bitterness, there's no room left for love.

Today, search your heart for all the people whom you have not yet forgiven. And forgive them. After all, when it comes to forgiveness, there's no time like the present. It's always the right time—and it's never too late—to do the right thing.

A Heart of Forgiveness

Today, think about the people you still need to forgive. And then ask God to help you forgive them.

Sin is largely a matter of mistaken priorities. Any sin in us that is cherished, hidden, and not confessed will cut the nerve center of our faith.

Catherine Marshall

The moment you wake up each morning, all your wishes and hopes for the day rush at you like wild animals. And the first job each morning consists in shoving it all back; in listening to that other voice, taking that other point of view, letting that other, larger, stronger, quieter life coming flowing in.

C. S. Lewis

How important it is for us—young and old—to live as if Jesus would return any day—to set our goals, make our choices, raise our children, and conduct business with the perspective of the imminent return of our Lord.

Gloria Gaither

Today's Prayer

Dear Lord, today is a new day. Help me finish the important tasks first, even if those tasks are difficult. Don't let me put off until tomorrow what I should do today. Amen

Pray for Perspective

So if you have been raised with the Messiah, seek what is above, where the Messiah is, seated at the right hand of God.

Colossians 3:1 HCSB

If a temporary loss of perspective has left you worried, exhausted, or both, it's time to readjust your thought patterns. Negative thoughts are habit-forming; thankfully, so are positive ones. With practice, you can form the habit of focusing on God's priorities and your own possibilities. When you do, you'll soon discover that you will spend less time fretting about your challenges and more time praising God for His gifts.

When you call upon the Lord and prayerfully seek His will, He will give you wisdom and perspective. When you make God's priorities your priorities, He will direct your steps and calm your fears. So today and every day hereafter, pray for a sense of balance and perspective. And remember: no problems are too big for God—and that includes yours.

Seeking God's Wisdom

When you focus on the world, you lose perspective. When you focus on God's promises, you gain a clearer perspective.

Attitude is the mind's paintbrush; it can color any situation.

Barbara Johnson

Like a shadow declining swiftly...away...like the dew of the morning gone with the heat of the day; like the wind in the treetops, like a wave of the sea, so are our lives on earth when seen in light of eternity.

Ruth Bell Graham

Instead of being frustrated and overwhelmed by all that is going on in our world, go to the Lord and ask Him to give you His eternal perspective.

Kay Arthur

The proper perspective creates within us a spirit of reaching outside of ourselves with joy and enthusiasm.

Luci Swindoll

Today's Prayer

Dear Lord, give me wisdom and perspective. Guide me according to Your plans for my life and according to Your commandments. And keep me mindful, Dear Lord, that Your truth is—and will forever be—the ultimate truth. Amen

Very Big Plans

Teach me to do Your will, for You are my God. May Your gracious Spirit lead me on level ground.

Psalm 143:10 HCSB

God has big plans for you. Your challenge is straightforward: discern His path and follow it. But beware: bitterness can get in the way.

Bitterness is a roadblock on the path that God has planned for your life. If you allow yourself to become resentful, discouraged, envious, or embittered, you will become "spiritually stuck." But, if you obey God's Word and forgive those who have harmed you, you will experience God's peace as you follow His path.

If you seek to live in accordance with God's will for your life—and you should—then you will live in accordance with His commandments. And don't forget: for Christians, forgiving others is never optional; forgiveness is required.

God intends to use you in wonderful, unexpected ways if you let Him. The decision to seek God's plan and to follow it is yours and yours alone. Don't let bitterness, or any other sin, get in the way.

Who is the person who fears the Lord? He will show him the way he should choose. He will live a good life, and his descendants will inherit the land.

Psalm 25:12-13 HCSB

We know that all things work together for the good of those who love God: those who are called according to His purpose.

Romans 8:28 HCSB

The steps of the Godly are directed by the Lord. He delights in every detail of their lives. Though they stumble, they will not fall, for the Lord holds them by the hand.

Psalm 37:23-24 NLT

For it is God who is working among you both the willing and the working for His good purpose.

Philippians 2:13 HCSB

A Heart of Forgiveness

God has a plan for your life, a plan that looks to the future, not the past. Your job is to make peace with the past and then look boldly to the future.

When the dream of our heart is one that God has planted there, a strange happiness flows into us. At that moment, all of the spiritual resources of the universe are released to help us. Our praying is then at one with the will of God and becomes a channel for the Creator's purposes for us and our world.

Catherine Marshall

Let's never forget that some of God's greatest mercies are His refusals. He says no in order that He may, in some way we cannot imagine, say yes. All His ways with us are merciful. His meaning is always love.

Elisabeth Elliot

Our souls were made to live in an upper atmosphere, and we stifle and choke if we live on any lower level. Our eyes were made to look off from these heavenly heights, and our vision is distorted by any lower gazing.

Hannah Whitall Smith

Today's Prayer

Dear Lord, I am Your creation, and You created me for a reason. Give me the wisdom to follow Your direction for my life's journey. Let me do Your work here on earth by seeking Your will and living it, knowing that when I trust in You, Father, I am eternally blessed. Amen

Bitterness Puts Distance Between You and God

Hatred stirs up conflicts, but love covers all offenses.

Proverbs 10:12 HCSB

Are you mired in the quicksand of bitterness or regret? If so, it's time to free yourself from the mire. The world holds few if any rewards for those who remain angrily focused upon the past. Still, the act of forgiveness is difficult for all but the most saintly men and women.

Being frail, fallible, imperfect human beings, most of us are quick to anger, quick to blame, slow to forgive, and even slower to forget. Yet we know that it's best to forgive others, just as we, too, have been forgiven.

If there exists even one person—including yourself—against whom you still harbor bitter feelings, it's time to forgive and move on. Bitterness, and regret are not part of God's plan for you, but God won't force you to forgive others. It's a job that only you can finish, and the sooner you finish it, the better.

A Heart of Forgiveness

You can never fully enjoy the present if you're bitter about the past. Instead of living in the past, make peace with it . . . and move on.

All bitterness, anger and wrath, insult and slander must be removed from you, along with all wickedness.
And be kind and compassionate to one another, forgiving one another, just as God also forgave you in Christ.

—

Ephesians 4:31-32 HCSB

Forgiveness is the key that unlocks the door of resentment and the handcuffs of hate. It is a power that breaks the chains of bitterness and the shackles of selfishness.

Corrie ten Boom

Bitterness is a spiritual cancer, a rapidly growing malignancy that can consume your life. Bitterness cannot be ignored but must be healed at the very core, and only Christ can heal bitterness.

Beth Moore

Grudges are like hand grenades; it is wise to release them before they destroy you.

Barbara Johnson

Sin is any deed or memory that hampers or binds human personality.

Catherine Marshall

Today's Prayer

Heavenly Father, free me from anger and bitterness. When I am angry, I cannot feel the peace that You intend for my life. When I am bitter, I cannot sense Your presence. Keep me mindful that forgiveness is Your commandment. Let me turn away from bitterness and instead claim the spiritual abundance that You offer through the gift of Your Son. Amen

Avoiding Needless Arguments

Starting a quarrel is like breaching a dam; so drop the matter before a dispute breaks out.

Proverbs 17:14 NIV

We live in a talk-show world where arguments are as plentiful as dandelion seeds on a windy spring day. But just because everybody else seems to be arguing doesn't mean that you need to join the chorus. A far better strategy is to learn when to offer constructive criticism and when to keep your trap shut.

Arguments, like criticism, come in at least two varieties: constructive and destructive. On occasion, arguments have positive outcomes, especially when those arguments are conducted by mature adults who are earnestly seeking the truth. Unfortunately, most arguments simply don't fit that description.

The next time you feel tempted to give someone "a piece of your mind" ask yourself which piece. Is it a piece of your anger or your insight? If the answer is the later, then you're free to speak up and share your enlightenment with the world. But, if the answer is the former, think twice before you vent. Since angry words, once spoken, can't be retrieved, it's better to think long and hard before you rant and rave . . . unless, of course, you're a talk radio host or a professional wrestler.

The words you speak are more important than you may realize. Your words have echoes that extend beyond the here and now. That's why you should seek to be an enlightenment and encouragement to others, not a constant critic or an angry adversary.

So avoid anguished outpourings. Suppress your impulsive outbursts. Curb the need to criticize. Terminate tantrums. Learn to speak words that lift others up as you share a message of encouragement and hope to a world that needs both.

When you talk, choose the very same words that you would use if your Savior were listening to your every word. Because He is.

A Heart of Forgiveness

Feeling the need to win the war of words is usually a matter of ego, not enlightenment. The next time you feel the urge for verbal combat, ask yourself if the exchange will be worth the time or energy. If not, forgive the other person and walk away.

Whatever you do when conflicts arise, be wise. Fight against jumping to quick conclusions and seeing only your side. There are always two sides on the streets of conflict. Look both ways.

Charles Swindoll

When you "win" an argument, what have you really won? Not much!

Marie T. Freeman

The Gospel has to be experienced, not argued!

Grady Nutt

Some fights are lost even though we win. A bulldog can whip a skunk, but it just isn't worth it.

Vance Havner

You don't have to attend every argument you're invited to!

Anonymous

Today's Prayer

Dear Lord, when I am tempted to be argumentative, keep me calm. When I fall prey to pettiness, restore my sense of perspective. When I am gripped by irrational anger, give me serenity. Let me show my thankfulness to You by offering forgiveness to others. And, when I do, may others see Your love reflected through my words and my deeds. Amen

Be a Joyful Christian

Make me hear joy and gladness.

Psalm 51:8 NKJV

Barbara Johnson says, "You have to look for the joy. Look for the light of God that is hitting your life, and you will find sparkles you didn't know were there."

Have you experienced that kind of joy? Hopefully so, because it's not enough to hear someone else talk about being joyful—you must actually experience that kind of joy in order to understand it.

Should you expect to be a joy-filled woman 24 hours a day, seven days a week, from this moment on? No. But you can (and should) experience pockets of joy frequently—that's the kind of joy-filled life that a woman like you deserves to live.

Guard Your Heart

Every day, God gives you cause to rejoice. And the rest is up to you.

What is your focus today? Joy comes when it is Jesus first, others second…then you.

Kay Arthur

The Christian lifestyle is not one of legalistic do's and don'ts, but one that is positive, attractive, and joyful.

Vonette Bright

If you're a thinking Christian, you will be a joyful Christian.

Marie T. Freeman

There may be no trumpet sound or loud applause when we make a right decision, just a calm sense of resolution and peace.

Gloria Gaither

Jesus did not promise to change the circumstances around us. He promised great peace and pure joy to those who would learn to believe that God actually controls all things.

Corrie ten Boom

Today's Prayer

Dear Lord, You have given me so many blessings, starting with my family. I will keep joy in my heart as I thank You, Lord, for every single blessing You've given me. Amen

Forgiveness and Perseverance

For you need endurance, so that after you have done God's will, you may receive what was promised.

Hebrews 10:36 HCSB

Life would be much simpler if we could forgive people "once and for all" and be done with it. But forgiveness is seldom that easy. For most of us, the decision to forgive is straightforward, but the process of forgiving is more difficult. Forgiveness is a journey that requires effort, time, perseverance, and prayer.

In a world filled with roadblocks and stumbling blocks, we need courage and perseverance. And, as an example of perfect perseverance, we need look no further than our Savior, Jesus Christ. Jesus finished what He began. Despite the torture He endured, despite the shame of the cross, Jesus never stopped loving, and He never stopped forgiving. As followers of Christ, we must, to the best of our abilities, follow in His footsteps.

If you are imprisoned by the chains of anger and bitterness, it's time to embark upon a journey of forgiveness. You can begin that journey by redirecting your thoughts and your prayers. If you sincerely wish to forgive someone, pray for that person. And then pray for yourself by asking God to heal your heart. Don't expect forgiveness to be easy or quick, but rest assured: with God as your partner, you can forgive . . . and you will.

Guard Your Heart

Life is an exercise in perseverance. If you persevere, you win.

Brothers, I do not consider myself to have taken hold of it. But one thing I do: forgetting what is behind and reaching forward to what is ahead, I pursue as my goal the prize promised by God's heavenly call in Christ Jesus.

Philippians 3:13-14 HCSB

So we must not get tired of doing good, for we will reap at the proper time if we don't give up.

Galatians 6:9 HCSB

But thanks be to God, who gives us the victory through our Lord Jesus Christ. Therefore, my beloved brethren, be steadfast, immovable, always abounding in the work of the Lord, knowing that your labor is not in vain in the Lord.

1 Corinthians 15:57-58 NKJV

Your life is not a boring stretch of highway. It's a straight line to heaven. And just look at the fields ripening along the way. Look at the tenacity and endurance. Look at the grains of righteousness. You'll have quite a crop at harvest…so don't give up!

Joni Eareckson Tada

Failure is one of life's most powerful teachers. How we handle our failures determines whether we're going to simply "get by" in life or "press on."

Beth Moore

If things are tough, remember that every flower that ever bloomed had to go through a whole lot of dirt to get there.

Barbara Johnson

God never gives up on you, so don't you ever give up on Him.

Marie T. Freeman

Today's Prayer

Lord, when life is difficult, I am tempted to abandon hope in the future. But You are my God, and I can draw strength from You. Let me trust You, Father, in good times and in bad times. Let me persevere—even if my soul is troubled—and let me follow Your Son, Jesus Christ, this day and forever. Amen

Follow Your Conscience

Let us draw near with a true heart in full assurance of faith, our hearts sprinkled clean from an evil conscience and our bodies washed in pure water.

Hebrews 10:22 HCSB

God gave you a conscience for a very good reason: to make your path conform to His will. Billy Graham correctly observed, "Most of us follow our conscience as we follow a wheelbarrow. We push it in front of us in the direction we want to go." To do so, of course, is a profound mistake. Yet all of us, on occasion, have failed to listen to the voice that God planted in our hearts, and all of us have suffered the consequences.

Wise believers make it a practice to listen carefully to that quiet internal voice. Count yourself among that number. When your conscience speaks, listen and learn. In all likelihood, God is trying to get His message through. And in all likelihood, it is a message that you desperately need to hear.

Seeking God's Wisdom

That quiet little voice inside your head will guide you down the right path if you listen carefully. Very often, your conscience will actually tell you what God wants you to do. So listen, learn, and behave accordingly.

God desires that we become spiritually healthy enough through faith to have a conscience that rightly interprets the work of the Holy Spirit.

Beth Moore

If I am walking along the street with a very disfiguring hole in the back of my dress, of which I am in ignorance, it is certainly a very great comfort to me to have a kind friend who will tell me of it. And similarly, it is indeed a comfort to know that there is always abiding with me a divine, all-seeing Comforter, who will reprove me for all my faults and will not let me go on in a fatal unconsciousness of them.

Hannah Whitall Smith

My conscience is captive to the word of God.

Martin Luther

There is no pillow so soft as a clear conscience.

Old Saying

Today's Prayer

Dear Lord, You speak to me through the Bible, through teachers, and through friends. And, Father, You speak to me through that still, small voice that warns me when I stray from Your will. In these quiet moments and throughout the day, show me Your plan for my life, Lord, that I might serve You. Amen

Renewing Your Spirit

Create in me a clean heart, O God, and renew a steadfast spirit within me.

Psalm 51:10 NKJV

Bitterness saps your energy; genuine forgiveness renews your spirit. If you find yourself tired, discouraged, or worse, perhaps you need to ask God to help you forgive others (just as He has already forgiven you).

God intends that His children lead joyous lives filled with abundance and peace. But sometimes, abundance and peace seem very far away. It is in these dark moments that we must turn to God for renewal; when we do, He will restore us.

Are you embittered about the past? Turn your heart toward God in prayer. Are you spiritually depleted? Call upon fellow believers to support you, and call upon Christ to renew your spirit and your life. Do you sincerely want to forgive someone? Ask God to heal your heart. When you do, you'll discover that the Creator of the universe stands always ready and always able to create a new sense of wonderment and joy in you.

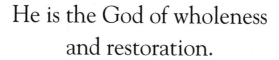

He is the God of wholeness and restoration.

Stormie Omartian

A Heart of Forgiveness

God can make all things new, including you. When you are weak or worried, God can renew your spirit. Your task is to let Him.

In those desperate times when we feel like we don't have an ounce of strength, He will gently pick up our heads so that our eyes can behold something—something that will keep His hope alive in us.

Kathy Troccoli

God specializes in things fresh and firsthand. His plans for you this year may outshine those of the past. He's prepared to fill your days with reasons to give Him praise.

Joni Eareckson Tada

Troubles we bear trustfully can bring us a fresh vision of God and a new outlook on life, an outlook of peace and hope.

Billy Graham

Today's Prayer

Dear Lord, You have the power to make all things new. When I grow weary, let me turn my thoughts and my prayers to You. When I am discouraged, restore my faith in You. Renew my strength, Father, and let me draw comfort and courage from Your promises and from Your unending love. Amen

Jesus Was a Servant
(And You Must Be, Too)

Be strong and of good courage, and do it; do not fear nor be dismayed, for the Lord God—my God—will be with you. He will not leave you nor forsake you, until you have finished all the work for the service of the house of the Lord.

1 Chronicles 28:20 NKJV

Jesus teaches that the most esteemed men and women are not the self-congratulatory leaders of society but are instead the humblest of servants. But, as weak human beings, we sometimes fall short as we seek to puff ourselves up and glorify our own accomplishments. To do so is wrong.

Today, you may feel the temptation to build yourself up in the eyes of your neighbors. Resist that temptation. Instead, serve your neighbors quietly and without fanfare. Find a need and fill it . . . humbly. Lend a helping hand and share a word of kindness . . . anonymously. This is God's way.

As a humble servant, you will glorify yourself, not before men, but before God, and that's what God intends. After all, earthly glory is fleeting: here today and all too soon gone. But, heavenly glory endures throughout eternity. So, the choice is yours: Either you can lift yourself up here on earth and be humbled in heaven, or vice versa.

A Heart for Service

The direction of your steps and the quality of your life will be determined by the level of your service.

God wants us to serve Him with a willing spirit, one that would choose no other way.

Beth Moore

In the very place where God has put us, whatever its limitations, whatever kind of work it may be, we may indeed serve the Lord Christ.

Elisabeth Elliot

If you want to discover your spiritual gifts, start obeying God. As you serve Him, you will find that He has given you the gifts that are necessary to follow through in obedience.

Anne Graham Lotz

Today's Prayer

Dear Lord, in weak moments, we may try to build ourselves up by placing ourselves ahead of others. But You want us to be humble servants to those who need our encouragement, our help, and our love. Today, we will do our best to follow in the footsteps of Your Son Jesus by serving others humbly, faithfully, and lovingly. Amen

Lasting Peace

Be of good comfort, be of one mind, live in peace; and the God of love and peace will be with you.

2 Corinthians 13:11 NKJV

Have you found the lasting peace that can—and should—be yours through Jesus Christ? Or are you still chasing the illusion of "peace and happiness" that the world promises but cannot deliver?

The beautiful words of John 14:27 promise that Jesus offers peace, not as the world gives, but as He alone gives: "Peace I leave with you. My peace I give to you. I do not give to you as the world gives. Your heart must not be troubled or fearful" (HCSB). Your challenge is to accept Christ's peace into your heart and then, as best you can, to share His peace with your neighbors. But sometimes, that's easier said than done.

If you are a person with lots of obligations and plenty of responsibilities, it is simply a fact of life: You worry. From time to time, you worry about finances, safety, health, home, family, or about countless other concerns, some great and some small. Where is the best place to take your worries? Take them to God . . . and leave them there.

The Scottish preacher George McDonald observed, "It has been well said that no man ever sank under the burden of the day. It is when tomorrow's burden is added to the burden of today that the weight is more than a man can bear. Never load yourselves so, my friends. If you find yourselves so loaded, at least remember this: it is your own doing, not God's. He begs you to leave the future to Him."

Today, as a gift to yourself, to your family, and to your friends, claim the inner peace that is your spiritual birthright: the peace of Jesus Christ. Christ is standing at the door, waiting patiently for you to invite Him to reign over your heart. His eternal peace is offered freely. Claim it today.

Guard Your Heart

God offers peace that passes human understanding . . . and He wants you to make His peace your peace.

The fruit of our placing all things in God's hands is the presence of His abiding peace in our hearts.

Hannah Whitall Smith

Today's Prayer

Dear Lord, the peace that the world offers is fleeting, but You offer a peace that is perfect and eternal. Let me take my concerns and burdens to You, Father, and let me feel the spiritual abundance that You offer through the person of Your Son, the Prince of Peace. Amen

Be a Practical Christian

Pure and undefiled religion before our God and Father is this: to look after orphans and widows in their distress and to keep oneself unstained by the world.

James 1:27 HCSB

What is "real" Christianity? Think of it as an on-going relationship—an all-encompassing relationship with God and with His Son Jesus. It is inevitable that your life must be lived in relationship to God. The question is not if you will have a relationship with Him; the burning question is whether that relationship will be one that seeks to honor Him or one that seeks to ignore Him.

We live in a world that discourages heartfelt devotion and obedience to God. Everywhere we turn, or so it seems, we are confronted by a mind-numbing assortment of distractions, temptations, obligations, and frustrations. Yet even on our busiest days, God beckons us to slow down and consult Him. When we do, we avail ourselves of the peace and abundance that only He can give.

A Heart of Forgiveness

If you sincerely wish to walk in Christ's footsteps, you must be willing to forgive those who have hurt you, just as He forgave those who hurt Him.

Every Christian is to become a little Christ. The whole purpose of becoming a Christian is simply nothing else.

C. S. Lewis

The Christian lifestyle is not one of legalistic do's and don'ts, but one that is positive, attractive, and joyful.

Vonette Bright

As you walk by faith, you live a righteous life, for righteousness is always by faith.

Kay Arthur

This life of faith, then, consists in just this—being a child in the Father's house. Let the ways of childish confidence and freedom from care, which so please you and win your heart when you observe your own little ones, teach you what you should be in your attitude toward God.

Hannah Whitall Smith

Faith has to be exercised in the midst of ordinary, down-to-earth living.

Elisabeth Elliot

Today's Prayer

Dear Lord, today, I will choose to please You and only You. I will obey Your commandments, and I will praise You for Your gifts, for Your Love, and for Your Son. Amen

You Don't Have to Be Perfect

The LORD is gracious and full of compassion, slow to anger and great in mercy. The LORD is good to all, and His tender mercies are over all His works.

Psalm 145:8-9 NKJV

Forgiveness is hard; complete forgiveness is even harder. Even if you are sincere in your desire to forgive someone and move on, you may find it difficult to make peace with the past. So, if you're trying to forgive someone but can't seem to do it, be patient. Pray about your feelings and ask God for His help. And then, when you've given it your best effort, be accepting of yourself, imperfect though you may be.

In heaven, you will know perfection. Here on earth, you have a few short years to wrestle with the challenges of imperfection. Remember this: you don't have to be perfect to be wonderful. In fact, you don't even need to be "almost-perfect". You simply must try your best and leave the rest up to God.

A Heart of Forgiveness

Don't worry about being perfect—it's impossible. God doesn't want your perfection; He wants your heart.

God is so inconceivably good. He's not looking for perfection. He already saw it in Christ. He's looking for affection.

Beth Moore

The happiest people in the world are not those who have no problems, but the people who have learned to live with those things that are less than perfect.

James Dobson

The greatest destroyer of good works is the desire to do great works.

C. H. Spurgeon

What makes a Christian a Christian is not perfection but forgiveness.

Max Lucado

Today's Prayer

Lord, this world has so many expectations of me, but today I will not seek to meet the world's expectations; I will do my best to meet Your expectations. I will make You my ultimate priority, Lord, by serving You, by praising You, by loving You, and by obeying You. Amen

Seek Fellowship

Then all the people began to eat and drink, send portions, and have a great celebration, because they had understood the words that were explained to them.

Nehemiah 8:12 HCSB

Fellowship with other believers should be an integral part of your everyday life. Your association with fellow Christians should be uplifting, enlightening, encouraging, and consistent.

Are you an active member of your own fellowship? Are you a builder of bridges inside the four walls of your church and outside it? Do you contribute to God's glory by contributing your time and your talents to a close-knit band of believers? Hopefully so. The fellowship of believers is intended to be a powerful tool for spreading God's Good News and uplifting His children. And God intends for you to be a fully contributing member of that fellowship. Your intentions should be the same.

Guard Your Heart

You need fellowship with men and women of faith. And your Christian friends need fellowship with you. So what are you waiting for?

Be united with other Christians. A wall with loose bricks is not good. The bricks must be cemented together.

Corrie ten Boom

One of the ways God refills us after failure is through the blessing of Christian fellowship. Just experiencing the joy of simple activities shared with other children of God can have a healing effect on us.

Anne Graham Lotz

In God's economy you will be hard-pressed to find many examples of successful "Lone Rangers."

Luci Swindoll

Christians are like coals of a fire. Together they glow—apart they grow cold.

Anonymous

When many men rejoice together, there is a richer job in each individual, since they enkindle themselves and they inflame one another.

St. Augustine

Today's Prayer

Heavenly Father, You have given me a community of supporters called the church. Let our fellowship be a reflection of the love we feel for each other and the love we feel for You. Amen

Don't Be Envious

Let us walk properly, as in the day, not in revelry and drunkenness, not in lewdness and lust, not in strife and envy.

Romans 13:13 NKJV

In a competitive, cut-throat world, it is easy to become envious of others' success. But it's wrong.

We know intuitively that envy is wrong, but because we are frail, imperfect human beings, we may find ourselves struggling with feelings of envy or resentment, or both. These feelings may be especially forceful when we see other people experience unusually good fortune.

Have you recently felt the pangs of envy creeping into your heart? If so, it's time to focus on the marvelous things that God has done for you and your family. And just as importantly, you must refrain from preoccupying yourself with the blessings that God has chosen to give others.

So here's a surefire formula for a happier, healthier life: Count your own blessings and let your neighbors count theirs. It's the godly way to live.

Guard Your Heart

Envy is a sin, a sin that robs you of contentment and peace. So you must refuse to let feelings of envy invade your thoughts or your heart.

Discontent dries up the soul.

Elisabeth Elliot

What God asks, does, or requires of others is not my business; it is His.

Kay Arthur

Too many Christians envy the sinners their pleasure and the saints their joy because they don't have either one.

Martin Luther

To love involves trusting the beloved beyond the evidence, even against much evidence. No man is our friend who believes in our good intentions only when they are proved. No man is our friend who will not be very slow to accept evidence against them. Such confidence, between one man and another, is in fact almost universally praised as a mortal beauty, not blamed as a logical error. And the suspicious man is blamed for a meanness of character, not admired for the excellence of his logic.

C. S. Lewis

Today's Prayer

Dear Lord, deliver me from the needless pain of envy. You have given me countless blessings. Let me be thankful for the gifts I have received, and let me never be resentful of the gifts You have given others. Amen

Turning Away from Anger

Don't let the sun go down on your anger, and don't give the Devil an opportunity.

Ephesians 4:26-27 HCSB

Anger is a natural human emotion that is sometimes necessary and appropriate. Even Jesus became angry when confronted with the moneychangers in the temple: "And Jesus entered the temple and drove out all those who were buying and selling in the temple, and overturned the tables of the moneychangers and the seats of those who were selling doves" (Matthew 21:12 NASB). Righteous indignation is an appropriate response to evil, but God does not intend that anger should rule our lives. Far from it. God intends that we turn away from anger whenever possible and forgive our neighbors as quickly as we can find it in our hearts to do so.

Life is full of frustrations: some great and some small. On occasion, you, like Jesus, will confront evil, and when you do, you may respond as He did: vigorously and without reservation. But more often than not, your frustrations will be of the more mundane variety. As long as you live here on earth, you will face countless opportunities to lose your temper over small, relatively insignificant events: a traffic jam, a spilled cup of coffee, an inconsiderate comment, or a broken promise.

When you are tempted to lose your temper over the minor inconveniences of life, don't. Turn away from anger, hatred, bitterness, and regret. Turn instead to God. And be quick to forgive the imperfections of His children. When you do, you will honor your Heavenly Father and you will give yourself a priceless gift…the gift of peace.

Guard Your Heart

Angry words are dangerous to your emotional and spiritual health, not to mention your relationships. So treat anger as an uninvited guest, and usher it away as quickly—and as quietly—as possible.

Life is too short to spend it being angry, bored, or dull.

Barbara Johnson

Anger breeds remorse in the heart, discord in the home, bitterness in the community, and confusion in the state.

Billy Graham

Today's Prayer

Dear Lord, help me to turn away from angry thoughts. Help me always to use Jesus as my guide for life, and let me trust His promises today and forever. Amen

On Guard Against Evil

Dear friend, do not imitate what is evil, but what is good. The one who does good is of God; the one who does evil has not seen God.

3 John 1:11 HCSB

This world is God's creation, and it contains the wonderful fruits of His handiwork. But, the world also contains countless opportunities to stray from God's will. Temptations are everywhere, and the devil, it seems, never takes a day off. Our task, as believers, is to turn away from temptation and to place our lives squarely in the center of God's will.

In his letter to Jewish Christians, Peter offered a stern warning: "Your adversary, the devil, prowls around like a roaring lion, seeking someone to devour" (1 Peter 5:8 NASB). What was true in New Testament times is equally true in our own. Evil is indeed abroad in the world, and Satan continues to sow the seeds of destruction far and wide. As Christians, we must guard our hearts by earnestly wrapping ourselves in the protection of God's Holy Word. When we do, we are protected.

Guard Your Heart

Evil exists, and it exists someplace not too far from you. You must guard your steps and your heart accordingly.

Where God's ministers are most successful, there the powers of darkness marshal their forces for the conflict.

Lottie Moon

We are in a continual battle with the spiritual forces of evil, but we will triumph when we yield to God's leading and call on His powerful presence in prayer.

Shirley Dobson

We actually are, at present, creatures whose character must be, in some respects, a horror to God, as it is, when we really see it, a horror to ourselves. This I believe to be a fact: and I notice that the holier a man is, the more fully he is aware of that fact.

C. S. Lewis

God judged it better to bring good out of evil than to suffer no evil to exist.

St. Augustine

Today's Prayer

Dear Lord, because You have given Your children free will, the world is a place where evil threatens our lives and our souls. Protect us, Father, from the evils and temptations of this difficult age. Help us to trust You, Father, and to obey Your Word, knowing that Your ultimate victory over evil is both inevitable and complete. Amen

The Wisdom to Be Generous

Freely you have received, freely give.

Matthew 10:8 NKJV

The thread of generosity is woven—completely and inextricably—into the very fabric of Christ's teachings. As He sent His disciples out to heal the sick and spread God's message of salvation, Jesus offered this guiding principle: "Freely you have received, freely give" (Matthew 10:8 NIV). The principle still applies. If we are to be disciples of Christ, we must give freely of our time, our possessions, and our love.

Lisa Whelchel spoke for Christian women everywhere when she observed, "The Lord has abundantly blessed me all of my life. I'm not trying to pay Him back for all of His wonderful gifts; I just realize that He gave them to me to give away." All of us have been blessed, and all of us are called to share those blessings without reservation.

Today, make this pledge and keep it: Be a cheerful, generous, courageous giver. The world needs your help, and you need the spiritual rewards that will be yours when you share your possessions, your talents, and your time.

A Heart of Forgiveness

A generous heart is a forgiving heart.

*So let each one give as he purposes in
his heart, not grudgingly or of necessity;
for God loves a cheerful giver.*

—

2 Corinthians 9:7 NKJV

Just pray for a tough hide and a tender heart.

Ruth Bell Graham

What is your focus today? Joy comes when it is Jesus first, others second...then you.

Kay Arthur

We can't do everything, but can we do anything more valuable than invest ourselves in another?

Elisabeth Elliot

The measure of a life, after all, is not its duration but its donation.

Corrie ten Boom

All kindness and good deeds, we must keep silent. The result will be an inner reservoir of power.

Catherine Marshall

Today's Prayer

Father, Your gifts are priceless. You gave Your Son Jesus to save us, and Your motivation was love. I pray that the gifts I give to others will come from an overflow of my heart, and that they will echo the great love You have for all of Your children. Amen

Contagious Christianity

Therefore, everyone who will acknowledge Me before men, I will also acknowledge him before My Father in heaven.

Matthew 10:32 HCSB

Genuine, heartfelt Christianity can be highly contagious. When you've experienced the transforming power of God's love, you feel the need to share the Good News of His only begotten Son. So, whether you realize it or not, you can be sure that you are being led to share the story of your faith with family, with friends, and with the world.

Every believer, including you, bears responsibility for sharing God's Good News. And it is important to remember that you share your testimony through words and actions, but not necessarily in that order.

Today, don't be bashful or timid: Talk about Jesus and, while you're at it, show the world what it really means to follow Him. After all, the fields are ripe for the harvest, time is short, and the workers are surprisingly few. So share your story today because tomorrow may indeed be too late.

A Heart of Forgiveness

If you want to be more like Jesus, follow in His footsteps every day, obey His commandments every day, and share His never-ending love—every day.

The Christian lifestyle is not one of legalistic do's and don'ts, but one that is positive, attractive, and joyful.

Vonette Bright

To be a Christian means to forgive the inexcusable, because God has forgiven the inexcusable in you.

C. S. Lewis

The Holy Spirit testifies of Jesus. So when you are filled with the Holy Spirit, you speak about our Lord and really live to His honor.

Corrie ten Boom

Christianity, in its purest form, is nothing more than seeing Jesus. Christian service, in its purest form, is nothing more than imitating him who we see. To see his Majesty and to imitate him...that is the sum of Christianity.

Max Lucado

Today's Prayer

Thank You, Lord, for Your Son. His love is boundless, infinite, and eternal. Today, let me pause and reflect upon Christ's love for me, and let me share that love with all those who cross my path. And, as an expression of my love for Him, let me share Christ's saving message with a world that desperately needs His grace. Amen

Guard Your Heart and Mind

Guard your heart above all else, for it is the source of life. Don't let your mouth speak dishonestly, and don't let your lips talk deviously. Let your eyes look forward; fix your gaze straight ahead. Carefully consider the path for your feet, and all your ways will be established. Don't turn to the right or to the left; keep your feet away from evil.

Proverbs 4:23-27 HCSB

God's Word is clear: we are to guard our hearts "above all else," yet we live in world that encourages us to do otherwise.

You are near and dear to God. He loves you more than you can imagine, and He wants the very best for you. God wants you to discover the peace that passes understanding, and to find that peace, you must learn how to forgive the people who have hurt you.

Every day, you are faced with choices . . . more choices than you can count. You can do the right thing, or not. You can be prudent, or not. You can be kind, and forgiving, and obedient to God. Or not.

Today, the world will offer you countless opportunities to let down your guard and, by doing so, make needless mistakes that may injure you or your loved ones. So be watchful and obedient. Guard your heart by giving it to your Heavenly Father; it is safe with Him.

Guard Your Heart

You should do whatever it takes to guard your heart—and with God's help, you can do it!

Becoming pure is a process of spiritual growth, and taking seriously the confession of sin during prayer time moves that process along, causing us to purge our life of practices that displease God.

Elizabeth George

He doesn't need an abundance of words. He doesn't need a dissertation about your life. He just wants your attention. He wants your heart.

Kathy Troccoli

We look at our burdens and heavy loads, and we shrink from them. But, if we lift them and bind them about our hearts, they become wings, and on them we can rise and soar toward God.

Mrs. Charles E. Cowman

Today's Prayer

Dear Lord, I will guard my heart against the evils, the temptations, and the distractions of this world. I will focus, instead, upon Your love, Your blessings, and Your Son. Amen

Answering the Call

I urge you now to live the life to which God called you.

Ephesians 4:1 NKJV

God is calling you to follow a specific path that He has chosen for your life. And it is vitally important that you heed that call. Otherwise, your talents and opportunities may go unused.

Have you already heard God's call? And are you pursuing it with vigor? If so, you're both fortunate and wise. But if you have not yet discovered what God intends for you to do with your life, keep searching and keep praying until you discover why the Creator put you here.

Remember: God has important work for you to do—work that no one else on earth can accomplish but you. The Creator has placed you in a particular location, amid particular people, with unique opportunities to serve. And He has given you all the tools you need to succeed. So listen for His voice, watch for His signs, and prepare yourself for the call that is sure to come.

Seeking God's Wisdom

God has a plan for your life, a divine calling that you can either answer or ignore. How you choose to respond to God's calling will determine the direction you take and the contributions you make.

If God has called you, do not spend time looking over your shoulder to see who is following you.

Corrie ten Boom

He treats us as sons, and all He asks in return is that we shall treat Him as a Father whom we can trust without anxiety. We must take the son's place of dependence and trust, and we must let Him keep the father's place of care and responsibility.

Hannah Whitall Smith

God never calls without enabling us. In other words, if he calls you to do something, he makes it possible for you to do it.

Luci Swindoll

There is wonderful freedom and joy in coming to recognize that the fun is in the becoming.

Gloria Gaither

Today's Prayer

Heavenly Father, You have called me, and I acknowledge that calling. In these quiet moments before this busy day unfolds, I come to You. I will study Your Word and seek Your guidance. Give me the wisdom to know Your will for my life and the courage to follow wherever You may lead me, today and forever. Amen

Passionate About Your Path

Whatever you do, do it enthusiastically, as something done for the Lord and not for men.

Colossians 3:23 HCSB

Do you see each day as a glorious opportunity to serve God and to do His will? Are you enthused about life, or do you struggle through each day giving scarcely a thought to God's blessings? Are you constantly praising God for His gifts, and are you sharing His Good News with the world? And are you excited about the possibilities for service that God has placed before you, whether at home, at work, at church, or at school? You should be.

You are the recipient of Christ's sacrificial love. Accept it enthusiastically and share it fervently. Jesus deserves your enthusiasm; the world deserves it; and you deserve the experience of sharing it.

Guard Your Heart

When you become genuinely enthused about your life and your faith, you'll guard your heart and improve your life.

Do not lack diligence;
be fervent in spirit; serve the Lord.

—

Romans 12:11 HCSB

God is the giver, and we are the receivers. And His richest gifts are bestowed not upon those who do the greatest things, but upon those who accept His abundance and His grace.

Hannah Whitall Smith

Living life with a consistent spiritual walk deeply influences those we love most.

Vonette Bright

Your light is the truth of the Gospel message itself as well as your witness as to Who Jesus is and what He has done for you. Don't hide it.

Anne Graham Lotz

We urgently need people who encourage and inspire us to move toward God and away from the world's enticing pleasures.

Jim Cymbala

Today's Prayer

Dear Lord, I know that others are watching the way that I live my life. Help me to be an enthusiastic Christian with a faith that is contagious. Amen

Be Disciplined

But I discipline my body and bring it into subjection, lest, when I have preached to others, I myself should become disqualified.

1 Corinthians 9:27 NKJV

Are you a self-disciplined woman? If so, congratulations . . . your disciplined approach to life can help you build a more meaningful relationship with God. Why? Because God expects all His believers (including you) to lead lives of disciplined obedience to Him . . . and He rewards those believers who do.

God doesn't reward disobedience, misbehavior, or apathy. So if you want to follow in the footsteps of God's Son, try becoming a more disciplined person. When you do, you'll be rewarded—richly rewarded—for your efforts.

Thoughtful women understand that God doesn't reward disobedience or misbehavior. To the contrary, God expects His children (of all ages) to lead disciplined lives . . . and when they do, He rewards them.

Seeking God's Wisdom

If you choose to obey God, your steps will be protected. If you choose to lead an undisciplined lifestyle, your steps will be misdirected.

Personal humility is a spiritual discipline and the hallmark of the service of Jesus.

Franklin Graham

We set our eyes on the finish line, forgetting the past, and straining toward the mark of spiritual maturity and fruitfulness.

Vonette Bright

God has a present will for your life. It is neither chaotic nor utterly exhausting. In the midst of many good choices vying for your time, He will give you the discernment to recognize what is best.

Beth Moore

It's sobering to contemplate how much time, effort, sacrifice, compromise, and attention we give to acquiring and increasing our supply of something that is totally insignificant in eternity.

Anne Graham Lotz

Today's Prayer

Dear Lord, make me a woman of discipline and righteousness. Let my conduct show others what it means to be a faithful Christian, and let me follow Your will and Your Word, today and every day. Amen

Trust God's Promises

For you need endurance, so that after you have done God's will, you may receive what was promised.

Hebrews 10:36 HCSB

What do you expect from the day ahead? Are you expecting God to do wonderful things, or are you living beneath a cloud of apprehension and doubt? The familiar words of Psalm 118:24 remind us of a profound yet simple truth: "This is the day which the LORD hath made; we will rejoice and be glad in it" (KJV).

For Christian believers, every day begins and ends with God's Son and God's promises. When we accept Christ into our hearts, God promises us the opportunity for earthly peace and spiritual abundance. But more importantly, God promises us the priceless gift of eternal life.

As we face the inevitable challenges of life here on earth, we must arm ourselves with the promises of God's Holy Word. When we do, we can expect the best, not only for the day ahead, but also for all eternity.

Seeking God's Wisdom

God has made many promises to you, and He will keep every single one of them. Your job is to trust God's promises and live accordingly.

God will never let you sink under your circumstances. He always provide a safety net and His love always encircles.

Barbara Johnson

Only believe, don't fear. Our Master, Jesus, always watches over us, and no matter what the persecution, Jesus will surely overcome it.

Lottie Moon

Our future may look fearfully intimidating, yet we can look up to the Engineer of the Universe, confident that nothing escapes His attention or slips out of the control of those strong hands.

Elisabeth Elliot

Worries carry responsibilities that belong to God, not to you. Worry does not enable us to escape evil; it makes us unfit to cope with it when it comes.

Corrie ten Boom

Today's Prayer

Lord, Your Holy Word contains promises, and I will trust them. I will use the Bible as my guide, and I will trust You, Lord, to speak to me through Your Holy Spirit and through Your Holy Word, this day and forever. Amen

Choosing to Have a Healthy Fear of God

Therefore, since we are receiving a kingdom that cannot be shaken, let us hold on to grace. By it, we may serve God acceptably, with reverence and awe.

Hebrews 12:28 HCSB

Are you a woman who possesses a healthy, fearful respect for God's power? Hopefully so. After all, God's Word teaches that the fear of the Lord is the beginning of knowledge (Proverbs 1:7).

When we fear the Creator—and when we honor Him by obeying His commandments—we receive God's approval and His blessings. But, when we ignore Him or disobey His commandments, we invite disastrous consequences.

God's hand shapes the universe, and it shapes our lives. God maintains absolute sovereignty over His creation, and His power is beyond comprehension. The fear of the Lord is, indeed, the beginning of knowledge. But thankfully, once we possess a healthy, reverent fear of God, we need never be fearful of anything else.

Guard Your Heart

If you have a healthy fear of God, you're wise—if you don't, you're not.

It is not possible that mortal men should be thoroughly conscious of the divine presence without being filled with awe.

C. H. Spurgeon

A healthy fear of God will do much to deter us from sin.

Charles Swindoll

The remarkable thing about fearing God is that when you fear God, you fear nothing else, whereas if you do not fear God, you fear everything else.

Oswald Chambers

When true believers are awed by the greatness of God and by the privilege of becoming His children, then they become sincerely motivated, effective evangelists.

Bill Hybels

I'm convinced that there is nothing that can happen to me in this life that is not precisely designed by a sovereign Lord to give me the opportunity to learn to know Him.

Elisabeth Elliot

Today's Prayer

Dear Lord, let my greatest fear be the fear of displeasing You. I will strive, Father, to obey Your commandments and seek Your will this day and every day of my life. Amen

When You Have Doubts

Now if any of you lacks wisdom, he should ask God, who gives to all generously and without criticizing, and it will be given to him. But let him ask in faith without doubting. For the doubter is like the surging sea, driven and tossed by the wind.

James 1:5-6 HCSB

I f you've never had any doubts about your faith, then you can stop reading this page now and skip to the next. But if you've ever been plagued by doubts about your faith or your God, keep reading.

Even some of the most faithful Christians are, at times, beset by occasional bouts of discouragement and doubt. But even when we feel far removed from God, God is never far removed from us. He is always with us, always willing to calm the storms of life—always willing to replace our doubts with comfort and assurance.

Whenever you're plagued by doubts, that's precisely the moment you should seek God's presence by genuinely seeking to establish a deeper, more meaningful relationship with His Son. Then you may rest assured that in time, God will calm your fears, answer your prayers, and restore your confidence.

Seeking God's Wisdom

When you have fears or doubts, don't ignore them. Talk to family, to friends, and, most importantly, to God.

We are most vulnerable to the piercing winds of doubt when we distance ourselves from the mission and fellowship to which Christ has called us.

Joni Eareckson Tada

Disobedience to His Word will cause you to doubt.

Anne Graham Lotz

Fear and doubt are conquered by a faith that rejoices. And faith can rejoice because the promises of God are as certain as God Himself.

Kay Arthur

Today's Prayer

Dear God, sometimes this world can be a puzzling place, filled with uncertainty and doubt. When I am unsure of my next step, keep me mindful that You are always near and that You can overcome any challenge. Give me faith, Father, and let me remember always that with Your love and Your power, I can live courageously and faithfully today and every day. Amen

Considering the Cross

But God forbid that I should boast except in the cross of our Lord Jesus Christ, by whom the world has been crucified to me, and I to the world.

Galatians 6:14 NKJV

As we consider Christ's sacrifice on the cross, we should be profoundly humbled and profoundly grateful. And today, as we come to Christ in prayer, we should do so in a spirit of quiet, heartfelt devotion to the One who gave His life so that we might have life eternal.

He was the Son of God, but He wore a crown of thorns. He was the Savior of mankind, yet He was put to death on a roughhewn cross made of wood. He offered His healing touch to an unsaved world, and yet the same hands that had healed the sick and raised the dead were pierced with nails.

Christ humbled Himself on a cross—for you. He shed His blood—for you. He has offered to walk with you through this life and throughout all eternity. As you approach Him today in prayer, think about His sacrifice and His grace. And be humble.

Guard Your Heart

The salvation that Jesus provided on the cross is free to us, but it cost Him so much. We must never take His sacrifice for granted.

Jesus came down from heaven, revealing exactly what God is like, offering eternal life and a personal relationship with God, on the condition of our rebirth—a rebirth made possible through His own death on the cross.

Anne Graham Lotz

God is my Heavenly Father. He loves me with an everlasting love. The proof of that is the Cross.

Elisabeth Elliot

The cross takes care of the past. The cross takes care of the flesh. The cross takes care of the world.

Kay Arthur

Today's Prayer

Dear Jesus, You are my Savior and my protector. You suffered on the cross for me, and I will give You honor and praise every day of my life. I will honor You with my words, my thoughts, and my prayers. And I will live according to Your commandments, so that through me, others might come to know Your perfect love. Amen

Stewardship of God's Gifts

Based on the gift they have received, everyone should use it to serve others, as good managers of the varied grace of God.

1 Peter 4:10 HCSB

The gifts that you possess are gifts from the Giver of all things good. Do you have a spiritual gift? Share it. Do you have a testimony about the things that Christ has done for you? Don't leave your story untold. Do you possess financial resources? Share them. Do you have particular talents? Hone your skills and use them for God's glory.

When you hoard the treasures that God has given you, you live in rebellion against His commandments. But, when you obey God by sharing His gifts freely and without fanfare, you invite Him to bless you more and more. Today, be a faithful steward of your talents and treasures. And then prepare yourself for even greater blessings that are sure to come.

A Heart for Service

God has given you a unique array of talents and opportunities. The rest is up to you.

The Lord has abundantly blessed me all of my life. I'm not trying to pay Him back for all of His wonderful gifts; I just realize that He gave them to me to give away.

Lisa Whelchel

When God crowns our merits, he is crowning nothing other than his gifts.

St. Augustine

If I find in myself a desire which no experience in this world can satisfy, the most probable explanation is that I was made for another world.

C. S. Lewis

If you want to discover your spiritual gifts, start obeying God. As you serve Him, you will find that He has given you the gifts that are necessary to follow through in obedience.

Anne Graham Lotz

Today's Prayer

Dear Lord, let me use my gifts, and let me help my family and friends discover theirs. Your gifts are priceless and eternal. May we, Your children, use them to the glory of Your kingdom, today and forever. Amen

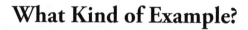

What Kind of Example?

Be an example to the believers in word, in conduct, in love, in spirit, in faith, in purity.

1 Timothy 4:12 NKJV

Whether we like it or not, all of us are role models. Our friends and family members watch our actions and, as followers of Christ, we are obliged to act accordingly.

What kind of example are you? Are you the kind of woman whose life serves as a genuine example of forgiveness and discipline? Are you a woman whose behavior serves as a positive role model for young people? Are you the kind of woman whose actions, day in and day out, are based upon kindness, faithfulness, and a love for the Lord? If so, you are not only blessed by God, but you are also a powerful force for good in a world that desperately needs positive influences such as yours.

A Heart of Forgiveness

When it comes to forgiveness, God wants you to be a positive role model. And that's what you should want, too.

*Set an example of good works yourself,
with integrity and dignity in your teaching.*

—

Titus 2:7 HCSB

Your light is the truth of the Gospel message itself as well as your witness as to Who Jesus is and what He has done for you. Don't hide it.

Anne Graham Lotz

Living life with a consistent spiritual walk deeply influences those we love most.

Vonette Bright

In your desire to share the gospel, you may be the only Jesus someone else will ever meet. Be real and be involved with people.

Barbara Johnson

Our trustworthiness implies His trustworthiness.

Beth Moore

There is nothing anybody else can do that can stop God from using us…We can turn everything into a testimony.

Corrie ten Boom

Today's Prayer

Dear Lord, help me be a worthy example to my friends and to my family. Let the things that I say and the things that I do show everyone what it means to be a follower of Your Son. Amen

Big Dreams

With God's power working in us, God can do much, much more than anything we can ask or imagine.

Ephesians 3:20 NCV

Are you willing to entertain the possibility that God has big plans in store for you? Hopefully so. Yet sometimes, especially if you've recently experienced a life-altering disappointment, you may find it difficult to envision a brighter future for yourself and your family. If so, it's time to reconsider your own capabilities . . . and God's.

Your Heavenly Father created you with unique gifts and untapped talents; your job is to tap them. When you do, you'll begin to feel an increasing sense of confidence in yourself and in your future.

It takes courage to dream big dreams. You will discover that courage when you do three things: accept the past, trust God to handle the future, and make the most of the time He has given you today.

Nothing is too difficult for God, and no dreams are too big for Him—not even yours. So start living—and dreaming—accordingly.

Seeking God's Wisdom

You can dream big dreams, but you can never out-dream God. His plans for you are even bigger than you can imagine.

Allow your dreams a place in your prayers and plans. God-given dreams can help you move into the future He is preparing for you.

Barbara Johnson

Sometimes our dreams were so big that it took two people to dream them.

Marie T. Freeman

If all things are possible with God, then all things are possible to him who believes in him.

Corrie ten Boom

Today's Prayer

Dear Lord, give me the courage to dream and the faithfulness to trust in Your perfect plan. When I am worried or weary, give me strength for today and hope for tomorrow. Keep me mindful of Your healing power, Your infinite love, and Your eternal salvation. Amen

Get Involved in a Church

And I also say to you that you are Peter, and on this rock I will build My church, and the forces of Hades will not overpower it. I will give you the keys of the kingdom of heaven, and whatever you bind on earth will have been bound in heaven, and whatever you loose on earth will have been loosed in heaven.

Matthew 16:18-19 HCSB

If you want to build a better life, the church is a wonderful place to do it. Are you an active, contributing, member of your local fellowship? The answer to this simple question will have a profound impact on the direction of your spiritual journey and the content of your character.

If you are not currently engaged in a local church, you're missing out on an array of blessings that include, but are certainly not limited to, the life-lifting relationships that you can—and should—be experiencing with fellow believers.

So do yourself a favor: Find a congregation you're comfortable with, and join it. And once you've joined, don't just attend church out of habit. Go to church out of a sincere desire to know and worship God. When you do, you'll be blessed by the men and women who attend your fellowship, and you'll be blessed by your Creator.

Guard Your Heart

God intends for you to be actively involved in His church. Your intentions should be the same.

Our churches are meant to be havens where the caste rules of the world do not apply.

Beth Moore

Be filled with the Holy Spirit; join a church where the members believe the Bible and know the Lord; seek the fellowship of other Christians; learn and be nourished by God's Word and His many promises. Conversion is not the end of your journey—it is only the beginning.

Corrie ten Boom

Someone has said that the Church at its very worst is better than the world at its best.

Gloria Gaither

Today's Prayer

Dear Lord, today I pray for Your church. Let me help to feed Your flock by helping to build Your church so that others, too, might experience Your enduring love and Your eternal grace. Amen

Thankful Forgiveness

Give thanks in all circumstances; for this is God's will for you in Christ Jesus.

1 Thessalonians 5:18 NIV

As believing Christians, we have every reason to thank God. But sometimes, when our hearts are troubled and our lives seem to be spinning out of control, we don't feel much like celebrating. Instead of thanking God for the blessings we have received, we waste time and energy fretting over the things we don't have. And, instead of forgiving those who have injured us, we seek revenge.

The words of 1 Thessalonians 5:18 remind us to give thanks in every circumstance of life. In all circumstances, our Father offers us His love, His strength, and His grace. And, in all circumstances, we must thank Him.

Have you thanked God today for blessings that are too numerous to count? Have you offered Him your heartfelt prayers and your wholehearted praise? If not, it's time to slow down and offer a prayer of thanksgiving to the One who has given you life on earth and life eternal.

If your heart is consumed with bitterness, there is no room left for thankfulness. But, if you are a thoughtful Christian, you will inevitably become a thankful Christian. No matter your circumstances, you owe God so much more than you can ever repay, and you owe Him your heartfelt thanks. So thank Him . . . and keep thanking Him, today, tomorrow and forever.

A Heart of Forgiveness

You owe God everything . . . including your gratitude and your obedience.

God is worthy of our praise and is pleased when we come before Him with thanksgiving.

Shirley Dobson

It is always possible to be thankful for what is given rather than to complain about what is not given. One or the other becomes a habit of life.

Elisabeth Elliot

Today's Prayer

Dear Lord, sometimes, amid the demands of the day, I lose perspective, and I fail to give thanks for Your blessings and for Your love. Today, help me to count those blessings, and let me give thanks to You, Father, for Your love, for Your grace, for Your blessings, and for Your Son. Amen

Studying God's Word

Like newborn infants, desire the unadulterated spiritual milk, so that you may grow by it in your salvation.

1 Peter 2:2 HCSB

As a spiritual being, you have the potential to grow in your personal knowledge of the Lord every day that you live. You can do so through prayer, through worship, through an openness to God's Holy Spirit, and through a careful study of God's Holy Word.

Your Bible contains powerful prescriptions for everyday living. If you sincerely seek to walk with God, you should commit yourself to the thoughtful study of His teachings. The Bible can and should be your roadmap for every aspect of your life.

Do you seek to establish a closer relationship with your Heavenly Father? Then study His Word every day, with no exceptions. The Holy Bible is a priceless, one-of-a-kind gift from God. Treat it that way and read it that way.

Seeking God's Wisdom

You're never too young—or too old—to become a serious student of God's Word.

Don't worry about what you do not understand of the Bible. Worry about what you do understand and do not live by.

Corrie ten Boom

The balance of affirmation and discipline, freedom and restraint, encouragement and warning is different for each child and season and generation, yet the absolutes of God's Word are necessary and trustworthy no matter how mercuric the time.

Gloria Gaither

The key to my understanding of the Bible is a personal relationship to Jesus Christ.

Oswald Chambers

The Bible is like no other book. Treat it that way!

Marie T. Freeman

If your Bible is falling apart, chances are your life is staying together.

Anonymous

Today's Prayer

Heavenly Father, Your Holy Word is a light unto my path. In all that I do, help me be a worthy witness for You as I share the Good News of Your perfect Son and Your perfect Word. Amen

Let God Judge

Do not judge, and you will not be judged. Do not condemn, and you will not be condemned. Forgive, and you will be forgiven.

Luke 6:37 HCSB

We have all fallen short of God's commandments, and He has forgiven us. We, too, must forgive others. And, we must refrain from judging them.

Are you one of those people who finds it easy to judge others? If so, it's time to change.

God does not need (or, for that matter, want) your help. Why? Because God is perfectly capable of judging the human heart . . . while you are not.

As Christians, we are warned that to judge others is to invite fearful consequences: to the extent we judge others, so, too, will we be judged by God. Let us refrain, then, from judging our neighbors. Instead, let us forgive them and love them in the same way that God has forgiven us.

A Heart of Forgiveness

If you're setting yourself up to be the judge and jury over other people, watch out! God will judge you in the same way you judge them. So don't be too hard on other people (unless, of course, you want God to be exactly that hard on you).

Judging draws the judgment of others.

Catherine Marshall

An individual Christian may see fit to give up all sorts of things for special reasons—marriage, or meat, or beer, or cinema; but the moment he starts saying these things are bad in themselves, or looking down his nose at other people who do use them, he has taken the wrong turn.

C. S. Lewis

Christians think they are prosecuting attorneys or judges, when, in reality, God has called all of us to be witnesses.

Warren Wiersbe

On judgment day you'll meet Father God—not Mother Earth!

Anonymous

Today's Prayer

Dear Lord, sometimes I am quick to judge others. But, You have commanded me not to judge. Keep me mindful, Father, that when I judge others, I am living outside of Your will for my life. You have forgiven me, Lord. Let me forgive others, let me love them, and let me help them . . . without judging them. Amen

Ask Him

So I say to you, ask, and it will be given to you; seek, and you will find; knock, and it will be opened to you. For everyone who asks receives, and he who seeks finds, and to him who knocks it will be opened.

Luke 11:9-10 NKJV

Have you fervently asked God to give you a forgiving heart? Have you asked Him for guidance, courage, and strength? If so, then you're continually inviting your Creator to reveal Himself in a variety of ways. As a follower of Christ, you must do no less.

Jesus made it clear to His disciples: they should petition God to meet their needs. So should we. Genuine, heartfelt prayer produces powerful changes in us and in our world. When we lift our hearts to God, we open ourselves to a never-ending source of divine wisdom and infinite love.

Do you have issues from your past that you can't seem to resolve? Do you have needs that you simply can't meet by yourself? Do you sincerely seek to know God's purpose for your life? If so, ask Him for direction, for protection, and for strength—and then keep asking Him every day that you live. Whatever your need, no matter how great or small, pray about it and never lose hope. God is not just near; He is here, and He's perfectly capable of answering your prayers. Now, it's up to you to ask.

A Heart of Forgiveness

If you sincerely want to forgive someone, ask for God's help. When you ask, He will answer.

Don't worry about anything, but in everything, through prayer and petition with thanksgiving, let your requests be made known to God.

Philippians 4:6 HCSB

Verily, verily, I say unto you, He that believeth on me, the works that I do shall he do also; and greater works than these shall he do; because I go unto my Father. And whatsoever ye shall ask in my name, that will I do, that the Father may be glorified in the Son. If ye shall ask any thing in my name, I will do it.

John 14:12-14 KJV

You did not choose Me, but I chose you. I appointed you that you should go out and produce fruit, and that your fruit should remain, so that whatever you ask the Father in My name, He will give you.

John 15:16 HCSB

When will we realize that we're not troubling God with our questions and concerns? His heart is open to hear us—his touch nearer than our next thought—as if no one in the world existed but us. Our very personal God wants to hear from us personally.

Gigi Graham Tchividjian

When trials come your way—as inevitably they will—do not run away. Run to your God and Father.

Kay Arthur

Often I have made a request of God with earnest pleadings even backed up with Scripture, only to have Him say "No" because He had something better in store.

Ruth Bell Graham

By asking in Jesus' name, we're making a request not only in His authority, but also for His interests and His benefit.

Shirley Dobson

Today's Prayer

Dear Lord, today I will ask You for the things I need. In every circumstance, in every season of life, I will come to You in prayer. You know the desires of my heart, Lord; grant them, I ask. Yet not my will, Father, but Your will be done. Amen

You and Your Family

But if any widow has children or grandchildren, they should learn to practice their religion toward their own family first and to repay their parents, for this pleases God.

1 Timothy 5:4 HCSB

As every woman knows, family life is a mixture of conversations, mediations, irritations, deliberations, commiserations, frustrations, negotiations and celebrations. In other words, the life of the typical woman is incredibly varied.

Certainly, in the life of every family, there are moments of frustration and disappointment. Lots of them. But, for those who are lucky enough to live in the presence of a close-knit, caring clan, the rewards far outweigh the frustrations. That's why we pray fervently for our family members, and that's why we love them despite their faults.

No family is perfect, and neither is yours. But, despite the inevitable challenges and occasional hurt feelings of family life, your clan is God's gift to you. That little band of men, women, kids, and babies is a priceless treasure on temporary loan from the Father above. Give thanks to the Giver for the gift of family…and act accordingly.

A Heart of Forgiveness

Your family is a precious gift from above, a gift that should be treasured, nurtured, and loved. Be quick to forgive your family members, just as God is quick to forgive you.

A home is a place where we find direction.

Gigi Graham Tchividjian

Living life with a consistent spiritual walk deeply influences those we love most.

Vonette Bright

Live in the present and make the most of your opportunities to enjoy your family and friends.

Barbara Johnson

The family that prays together, stays together.

Anonymous

Today's Prayer

Dear Lord, I am part of Your family, and I praise You for Your gifts and for Your love. You have also blessed me with my earthly family, and I pray for them, that they might be protected and blessed by You. Let me show love and acceptance for my family, Lord, so that through me, they might come to know and to love You. Amen

Be Still

Be still, and know that I am God.

Psalm 46:10 NKJV

We live in a noisy world, a world filled with distractions, frustrations, and complications. But if we allow the distractions of a clamorous world to separate us from God's peace, we do ourselves a profound disservice.

If we seek to maintain righteous minds and compassionate hearts, we must take time each day for prayer and for meditation. We must make ourselves still in the presence of our Creator. We must quiet our minds and our hearts so that we can sense God's will, God's love, and God's Son.

Are you one of those busy women who rush through the day with scarcely a single moment for quiet contemplation and prayer? If so, it's time to reorder your priorities. Nothing is more important than the time you spend with your Savior. So be still and claim the inner peace that is your spiritual birthright: the peace of Jesus Christ. It is offered freely; it has been paid for in full; it is yours for the asking. So ask. And then share.

Seeking God's Wisdom

Be still and listen to God. He has something important to say to you.

The manifold rewards of a serious, consistent prayer life demonstrate clearly that time with our Lord should be our first priority.

Shirley Dobson

The Lord Jesus, available to people much of the time, left them, sometimes a great while before day, to go up to the hills where He could commune in solitude with His Father.

Elisabeth Elliot

I need the spiritual revival that comes from spending quiet time alone with Jesus in prayer and in thoughtful meditation on His Word.

Anne Graham Lotz

Today's Prayer

Lord, Your Holy Word is a light unto the world; let me study it, trust it, and share it with all who cross my path. Let me discover You, Father, in the quiet moments of the day. And, in all that I say and do, help me to be a worthy witness as I share the Good News of Your perfect Son and Your perfect Word. Amen

Your Bright Future

"For I know the plans I have for you"—[this is] the Lord's declaration—"plans for [your] welfare, not for disaster, to give you a future and a hope."

Jeremiah 29:11 HCSB

Sometimes the future seems bright, and sometimes it does not. Yet even when we cannot see the possibilities of tomorrow, God can. Our challenge is to trust ourselves to do the best work we can, and then to trust God to do the rest.

If we stay focused on the past, we can't fully embrace the future. Of course, we all face disappointments and failures while we are here on earth, but these are only temporary defeats. This world can be a place of trials and tribulations, but when we place our trust in the Giver of all things good, we are secure. God has promised us peace, joy, and eternal life. And God keeps His promises today, tomorrow, and forever.

Are you willing to make peace with your past and to place your future in the hands of a loving and all-knowing God? Do you trust in the ultimate goodness of His plan for your life? Will you face today's challenges with optimism and hope? You should. After all, God created you for a very important purpose: His purpose. And you still have important work to do: His work.

Today, as you live in the present and look to the future, remember that God has a plan for you. Act—and believe—accordingly.

A Heart of Forgiveness

Even when the world seems dark, the future is bright for those who look to the Son.

We spend our lives dreaming of the future, not realizing that a little of it slips away every day.

Barbara Johnson

Do not limit the limitless God! With Him, face the future unafraid because you are never alone.

Mrs. Charles E. Cowman

Every experience God gives us, every person he brings into our lives, is the perfect preparation for the future that only he can see.

Corrie ten Boom

Today's Prayer

Dear Lord, as I look to the future, I will place my trust in You. If I become discouraged, I will turn to You. If I am afraid, I will seek strength in You. You are my Father, and I will place my hope, my trust, and my faith in You. Amen

Paying Attention to God

For where your treasure is, there your heart will be also.

Luke 12:34 HCSB

Who is in charge of your heart? Is it God, or is it something else? Have you given Christ your heart, your soul, your talents, your time, and your testimony? Or are you giving Him little more than a few hours each Sunday morning?

In the book of Exodus, God warns that we should place no gods before Him. Yet all too often, we place our Lord in second, third, or fourth place as we worship other things. When we unwittingly place possessions or relationships above our love for the Creator, we create big problems for ourselves.

Does God rule your heart? Make certain that the honest answer to this question is a resounding yes. In the life of every radical believer, God comes first. And that's precisely the place that He deserves in your heart.

Guard Your Heart

Because God is infinite and eternal, you cannot comprehend Him. But you can understand your need to praise Him, to love Him, and to obey His Word.

He treats us as sons, and all He asks in return is that we shall treat Him as a Father whom we can trust without anxiety. We must take the son's place of dependence and trust, and we must let Him keep the father's place of care and responsibility.

Hannah Whitall Smith

He is always thinking about us. We are before his eyes. The Lord's eye never sleeps, but is always watching out for our welfare. We are continually on his heart.

C. H. Spurgeon

In heaven, we will see that nothing, absolutely nothing, was wasted, and that every tear counted and every cry was heard.

Joni Eareckson Tada

God loves each of us as if there were only one of us.

St. Augustine

Today's Prayer

Your faithfulness, Lord, is everlasting. You are faithful to me even when I am not faithful to You. Today, let me serve You with my heart, my soul, and my mind. And, then, let me rest in the knowledge of Your unchanging and constant love for me. Amen

Directing Your Thoughts

Finally brothers, whatever is true, whatever is honorable, whatever is just, whatever is pure, whatever is lovely, whatever is commendable—if there is any moral excellence and if there is any praise—dwell on these things.

Philippians 4:8 HCSB

Christ forgave those who hurt Him, and we should do likewise. When we forgive others, we bring ourselves closer to the Savior; when we harbor bitterness in our hearts, we distance ourselves from Him.

Your life is a series of thoughts and actions. Each day, your thoughts and actions can bring you closer to God...or not. When you live according to God's commandments, you reap bountiful rewards: abundance, hope, and peace, for starters. But, if you turn your back upon God by disobeying Him, you invite bitter consequences.

Do you seek to walk in the footsteps of the One from Galilee, or will you choose another path? If you sincerely seek Christ's peace and His blessings, you must strive to imitate Him. Your Savior offered forgiveness to His enemies . . . now it's your turn.

Guard Your Heart

Either you can control your thoughts, or they most certainly will control you.

*Therefore, get your minds ready for
action, being self-disciplined,
and set your hope completely on the grace
to be brought to you
at the revelation of Jesus Christ.*

—

1 Peter 1:13 HCSB

As we have by faith said no to sin, so we should by faith say yes to God and set our minds on things above, where Christ is seated in the heavenlies.

Vonette Bright

No more imperfect thoughts. No more sad memories. No more ignorance. My redeemed body will have a redeemed mind. Grant me a foretaste of that perfect mind as you mirror your thoughts in me today.

Joni Eareckson Tada

It is the thoughts and intents of the heart that shape a person's life.

John Eldredge

Preoccupy my thoughts with your praise beginning today.

Joni Eareckson Tada

Today's Prayer

Dear Lord, I will focus on Your love, Your power, Your promises, and Your Son. When I am weak, I will turn to You for strength; when I am worried, I will turn to You for comfort; when I am troubled, I will turn to You for patience and perspective. Help me guard my thoughts, Lord, so that I may honor You this day and forever. Amen

Be Patient and Trust God

Be silent before the Lord and wait expectantly for Him.

Psalm 37:7 HCSB

Psalm 37:7 instructs us to wait patiently for God. But as busy women in a fast-paced world, many of us find that waiting quietly for God is difficult. Why? Because we are fallible human beings seeking to live according to our own timetables, not God's. In our better moments, we realize that patience is not only a virtue, but it is also a commandment from God.

We human beings are impatient by nature. We know what we want, and we know exactly when we want it: NOW! But, God knows better. He has created a world that unfolds according to His plans, not our own. As believers, we must trust His wisdom and His goodness.

God instructs us to be patient in all things. We must be patient with our families, our friends, and our associates. We must also be patient with our Creator as He unfolds His plan for our lives. And that's as it should be. After all, think how patient God has been with us.

A Heart of Forgiveness

When you learn to be more patient with others, you'll make your world—and your heart—a better place.

Let me encourage you to continue to wait with faith. God may not perform a miracle, but He is trustworthy to touch you and make you whole where there used to be a hole.

Lisa Whelchel

Wisdom always waits for the right time to act, while emotion always pushes for action right now.

Joyce Meyer

How do you wait upon the Lord? First you must learn to sit at His feet and take time to listen to His words.

Kay Arthur

When we read of the great Biblical leaders, we see that it was not uncommon for God to ask them to wait, not just a day or two, but for years, until God was ready for them to act.

Gloria Gaither

Today's Prayer

Lord, give me patience. When I am hurried, give me peace. When I am frustrated, give me perspective. When I am angry, let me turn my heart to You. Today, let me become a more patient woman, Dear Lord, as I trust in You and in Your master plan for my life. Amen

If You Reach Out to God . . .

Draw near to God, and He will draw near to you.

James 4:8 HCSB

Do you ever wonder if God is really "right here, right now"? Do you wonder if God hears your prayers, if He understands your feelings, or if He really knows your heart? If so, you're not alone: lots of very faithful Christians have experienced periods of doubt. In fact, some of the biggest heroes in the Bible had plenty of doubts—and so, perhaps, will you. But when you have doubts, remember this: God isn't on a coffee break, and He hasn't moved out of town. God isn't taking a long vacation, and He isn't snoozing on the couch. He's right here, right now, listening to your thoughts and prayers, watching over your every move.

If you'd like to get to know God a little bit better, He's always available—always ready to listen to your prayers, and always ready to speak to your heart. Are you ready to talk to Him? If so, congratulations. If not, what are you waiting for?

Seeking God's Wisdom

In order to know God more intimately, you should talk to Him more often. The more often you speak to Him, the more often He'll speak to you.

Knowing God involves an intimate, personal relationship that is developed over time through prayer and getting answers to prayer, through Bible study and applying its teaching to our lives, through obedience and experiencing the power of God, through moment-by-moment submission to Him that results in a moment-by-moment filling of the Holy Spirit.

Anne Graham Lotz

Here is our opportunity: we cannot see God, but we can see Christ. Christ was not only the Son of God, but He was the Father. Whatever Christ was, that God is.

Hannah Whitall Smith

The only way we can be convinced of Who Jesus is, is through the enlightenment we have received from the Holy Spirit.

Anne Graham Lotz

Today's Prayer

Dear Lord, give me the wisdom to seek You, the patience to wait for You, the insight to hear You, and the courage to obey You, this day and forever. Amen

Entrusting Your Hopes to God

You, Lord, give true peace to those who depend on you, because they trust you.

Isaiah 26:3 NCV

As every woman knows, hope is a perishable commodity. Despite God's promises, despite Christ's love, and despite our countless blessings, we frail human beings can still lose hope from time to time. When we do, we need the encouragement of Christian friends, the life-changing power of prayer, and the healing truth of God's Holy Word. If we find ourselves falling into the spiritual traps of worry and discouragement, we should seek the healing touch of Jesus and the encouraging words of fellow Christians. Even though this world can be a place of trials and struggles, God has promised us peace, joy, and eternal life if we give ourselves to Him.

Trusting God's Promises

Since God has promised to guide and protect you—now and forever—you should never lose hope.

*Let us hold on to the confession
of our hope without wavering,
for He who promised is faithful.*

—

Hebrews 10:23 HCSB

Never yield to gloomy anticipation. Place your hope and confidence in God. He has no record of failure.

Mrs. Charles E. Cowman

The best we can hope for in this life is a knothole peek at the shining realities ahead. Yet a glimpse is enough. It's enough to convince our hearts that whatever sufferings and sorrows currently assail us aren't worthy of comparison to that which waits over the horizon.

Joni Eareckson Tada

I discovered that sorrow was not to be feared but rather endured with hope and expectancy that God would use it to visit and bless my life.

Jill Briscoe

Love is the seed of all hope. It is the enticement to trust, to risk, to try, and to go on.

Gloria Gaither

Today's Prayer

Dear Lord, I will place my hope in You. If I become discouraged, I will turn to You. If I am afraid, I will seek strength in You. In every aspect of my life, I will trust You. You are my Father, and I will place my hope, my trust, and my faith in You. Amen

Have the Courage to Trust God

Trust in the Lord with all your heart, and do not rely on your own understanding; think about Him in all your ways, and He will guide you on the right paths.

Proverbs 3:5-6 HCSB

When our dreams come true and our plans prove successful, we find it easy to thank our Creator and easy to trust His divine providence. But in times of sorrow or hardship, we may find ourselves questioning God's plans for our lives.

On occasion, you will confront circumstances that trouble you to the very core of your soul. It is during these difficult days that you must find the wisdom and the courage to trust your Heavenly Father despite your circumstances.

Are you a woman who seeks God's blessings for yourself and your family? Then trust Him. Trust Him with your relationships. Trust Him with your priorities. Follow His commandments and pray for His guidance. Trust Your Heavenly Father day by day, moment by moment—in good times and in trying times. Then, wait patiently for God's revelations . . . and prepare yourself for the abundance and peace that will most certainly be yours when you do.

Trusting God's Promises

Because God is trustworthy—and because He has made promises to you that He intends to keep—you are protected.

Sometimes the very essence of faith is trusting God in the midst of things He knows good and well we cannot comprehend.

Beth Moore

Are you serious about wanting God's guidance to become the person he wants you to be? The first step is to tell God that you know you can't manage your own life; that you need his help.

Catherine Marshall

Never be afraid to trust an unknown future to a known God.

Corrie ten Boom

Today's Prayer

Dear Lord, let my faith be in You, and in You alone. Without You, I am weak, but when I trust You, I am protected. In every aspect of my life, Father, let me place my hope and my trust in Your infinite wisdom and Your boundless grace. Amen

Let God Guide the Way

The true children of God are those who let God's Spirit lead them.

Romans 8:14 NCV

The Bible promises that God will guide you if you let Him. Your job, of course, is to let Him. But sometimes, you will be tempted to do otherwise. Sometimes, you'll be tempted to go along with the crowd; other times, you'll be tempted to do things your way, not God's way. When you feel those temptations, resist them.

What will you allow to guide you through the coming day: your own desires (or, for that matter, the desires of your friends)? Or will you allow God to lead the way? The answer should be obvious. You should let God be your guide. When you entrust your life to Him completely and without reservation, God will give you the strength to meet any challenge, the courage to face any trial, and the wisdom to live in His righteousness. So trust Him today and seek His guidance. When you do, your next step will be the right one.

Seeking God's Wisdom

If you're wise, you'll allow God to guide you today and every day of your life. When you pray for guidance, God will give it.

The LORD says,
"I will guide you along the best
pathway for your life.
I will advise you and watch over you."

—

Psalm 32:8 NLT

God's guidance is even more important than common sense. I can declare that the deepest darkness is outshone by the light of Jesus.

Corrie ten Boom

We have ample evidence that the Lord is able to guide. The promises cover every imaginable situation. All we need to do is to take the hand he stretches out.

Elisabeth Elliot

Is God your spare wheel or your steering wheel?

Anonymous

It's a bit like river rafting with an experienced guide. You may begin to panic when the guide steers you straight into a steep waterfall, especially if another course appears much safer. Yet, after you've emerged from the swirling depths and wiped the spray from your eyes, you see that just beyond the seemingly "safe" route was a series of jagged rocks. Your guide knew what he was doing after all.

Shirley Dobson

Today's Prayer

Lord, You have a plan for my life. Let me discover it and live it. Today, I will seek Your will, knowing that when I trust in You, Dear Father, I am eternally blessed. Amen

Pray for God's Abundance

I have come that they may have life, and that they may have it more abundantly.

John 10:10 NKJV

The familiar words of John 10:10 should serve as a daily reminder: Christ came to this earth so that we might experience His abundance, His love, and His gift of eternal life. But Christ does not force Himself upon us; we must claim His gifts for ourselves.

Every woman knows that some days are so busy and so hurried that abundance seems like a distant promise. It is not. Every day, we can claim the spiritual abundance that God promises for our lives…and we should.

Hannah Whitall Smith spoke for believers of every generation when she observed, "God is the giver, and we are the receivers. And His richest gifts are bestowed not upon those who do the greatest things, but upon those who accept His abundance and His grace."

Christ is, indeed, the Giver. Will you accept His gifts today?

A Heart of Forgiveness

God wants to shower you with abundance—your job is to let Him.

The gift of God is eternal life, spiritual life, abundant life through faith in Jesus Christ, the Living Word of God.

Anne Graham Lotz

God's riches are beyond anything we could ask or even dare to imagine! If my life gets gooey and stale, I have no excuse.

Barbara Johnson

Yes, we were created for His holy pleasure, but we will ultimately—if not immediately—find much pleasure in His pleasure.

Beth Moore

It would be wrong to have a "poverty complex," for to think ourselves paupers is to deny either the King's riches or to deny our being His children.

Catherine Marshall

Today's Prayer

Dear Lord, thank You for the joyful, abundant life that is mine through Christ Jesus. Guide me according to Your will, and help me become a woman whose life is a worthy example to others. Give me courage, Lord, to claim the spiritual riches that You have promised, and show me Your plan for my life, today and forever. Amen

Trust God's Wisdom

Insight is a fountain of life for its possessor, but folly is the instruction of fools.

Proverbs 16:22 HCSB

Where will you place your trust today? Will you trust in the wisdom of fallible men and women, or will you place your faith in God's perfect wisdom? When you decide whom to trust, you will then know how best to respond to the challenges of the coming day.

Are you tired? Discouraged? Fearful? Be comforted and trust God. Are you worried or anxious? Be confident in God's power and trust His Holy Word. Are you confused? Listen to the quiet voice of your Heavenly Father. He is not a God of confusion. Talk with Him; listen to Him; trust Him. He is steadfast, and He is your Protector . . . forever.

Seeking God's Wisdom

God's wisdom is perfect, and it's available to you. So if you want to become wise, become a student of God's Word and a follower of His Son.

We get into trouble when we think we know what to do and we stop asking God if we're doing it.

Stormie Omartian

If you are struggling to make some difficult decisions right now that aren't specifically addressed in the Bible, don't make a choice based on what's right for someone else. You are the Lord's and He will make sure you do what's right.

Lisa Whelchel

Make God's will the focus of your life day by day. If you seek to please Him and Him alone, you'll find yourself satisfied with life.

Kay Arthur

The will of God is never exactly what you expect it to be. It may seem to be much worse, but in the end it's going to be a lot better and a lot bigger.

Elisabeth Elliot

Today's Prayer

Dear Lord, You are my Teacher. Help me to learn from You. And then, let me show others what it means to be a kind, generous, loving Christian. Amen

The Dangers of Pride

Pride comes before destruction, and an arrogant spirit before a fall.

Proverbs 16:18 HCSB

The words from Proverbs 16 remind us that pride and destruction are traveling partners. But as imperfect human beings, we are tempted to puff out our chests and crow about our own accomplishments. When we do so, we delude ourselves.

As Christians, we have a profound reason to be humble: We have been refashioned and saved by Jesus Christ, and that salvation came not because of our own good works but because of God's grace. Thus, we are not "self-made"; we are "God-made" and "Christ-saved." How, then, can we be boastful? The answer, of course, is simple: if we are honest with ourselves and with our God, we cannot be boastful. In the quiet moments, when we search the depths of our own hearts, we know that whatever "it" is, God did that. And He deserves the credit.

Guard Your Heart

All of your talents and abilities come from God. Give Him thanks, and give Him the glory.

All kindness and good deeds, we must keep silent. The result will be an inner reservoir of personality power.

Catherine Marshall

We cannot be filled until we are empty. We have to be poor in spirit of ourselves in order to be filled with the Holy Spirit.

Corrie ten Boom

It was as important to me that my children be no more self-righteous than they were unrighteous. In His Gospels, Christ seemed far more tolerant of a repentant sinner than a self-righteous, self-proclaimed saint.

Beth Moore

God exalts humility. When God works in our lives, helping us to become humble, he gives us a permanent joy. Humility gives us a joy that cannot be taken away.

Max Lucado

Today's Prayer

Lord, make me a woman with a humble heart. Keep me mindful, Dear God, that all my gifts come from You. Let me grow beyond my need for earthly praise, Lord, and when I seek approval, let me look only to You. Amen

The Decision to Celebrate Life

This is the day the Lord has made; let us rejoice and be glad in it.

Psalm 118:24 HCSB

For Christians, every day begins and ends with God and His Son. Christ came to this earth to give us abundant life and eternal salvation. We give thanks to our Maker when we treasure each day and use it to the fullest.

Today is God's gift to you. How you use it is your gift to God. So how do you plan to use today's gift? Will you celebrate God's blessings and obey His commandments? Will you share words of encouragement and hope with all who cross your path? Will you share the Good News of the risen Christ? Only you can answer these questions. May you answer wisely today and every day of your life.

Guard Your Heart

Every day should be a cause for celebration. By celebrating the gift of life, you protect your heart from the dangers of pessimism, regret, hopelessness, and bitterness.

Christ is the secret, the source,
the substance, the center,
and the circumference of
all true and lasting gladness.

—

Mrs. Charles E. Cowman

According to Jesus, it is God's will that His children be filled with the joy of life.

Catherine Marshall

If you can forgive the person you were, accept the person you are, and believe in the person you will become, you are headed for joy. So celebrate your life.

Barbara Johnson

When the dream of our heart is one that God has planted there, a strange happiness flows into us. At that moment, all of the spiritual resources of the universe are released to help us. Our praying is then at one with the will of God and becomes a channel for the Creator's purposes for us and our world.

Catherine Marshall

Joy is a by-product not of happy circumstances, education or talent, but of a healthy relationship with God and a determination to love Him no matter what.

Barbara Johnson

Today's Prayer

Dear Lord, help us remember that every day is a cause for celebration. Today we will try our best to keep joy in our hearts. We will celebrate the life You have given us here on earth and the eternal life that will be ours in heaven. Amen

Follow Him

If anyone serves Me, let him follow Me; and where I am, there My servant will be also. If anyone serves Me, him My Father will honor.

John 12:26 NKJV

Jesus walks with you. Are you walking with Him? Hopefully, you will choose to walk with Him today and every day of your life.

Jesus loved you so much that He endured unspeakable humiliation and suffering for you. How will you respond to Christ's sacrifice? Will you take up His cross and follow Him (Luke 9:23), or will you choose another path? When you place your hopes squarely at the foot of the cross, when you place Jesus squarely at the center of your life, you will be blessed. If you seek to be a worthy disciple of Jesus, you must acknowledge that He never comes "next." He is always first.

Do you hope to fulfill God's purpose for your life? Do you seek a life of abundance and peace? Do you intend to be Christian, not just in name, but in deed? Then follow Christ. Follow Him by picking up His cross today and every day that you live. When you do, you will quickly discover that Christ's love has the power to change everything, including you.

Then He said to them all, "If anyone wants to come with Me, he must deny himself, take up his cross daily, and follow Me."

Luke 9:23 HCSB

For I have given you an example that you also should do just as I have done for you.

John 13:15 HCSB

No one can be a slave of two masters, since either he will hate one and love the other, or be devoted to one and despise the other. You cannot be slaves of God and of money.

Matthew 6:24 HCSB

Anyone finding his life will lose it, and anyone losing his life because of Me will find it.

Matthew 10:39 HCSB

A Heart of Forgiveness

It takes genuine commitment—and significant sacrifices—to really follow Jesus. And it's worth it.

Peter said, "No, Lord!" But he had to learn that one cannot say "No" while saying "Lord" and that one cannot say "Lord" while saying "No."

Corrie ten Boom

Will you, with a glad and eager surrender, hand yourself and all that concerns you over into his hands? If you will do this, your soul will begin to know something of the joy of union with Christ.

Hannah Whitall Smith

The Christian faith is meant to be lived moment by moment. It isn't some broad, general outline—it's a long walk with a real Person. Details count: passing thoughts, small sacrifices, a few encouraging words, little acts of kindness, brief victories over nagging sins.

Joni Eareckson Tada

Today's Prayer

Dear Jesus, because I am Your disciple, I will trust You, I will obey Your teachings, and I will share Your Good News. You have given me life abundant and life eternal, and I will follow You today and forever. Amen

A Rule That's Golden

Therefore, whatever you want others to do for you, do also the same for them—this is the Law and the Prophets.

Matthew 7:12 HCSB

How should we treat other people? God's Word is clear: we should treat others in the same way that we wish to be treated. This Golden Rule is easy to understand but, at times, difficult to live by.

Because we are imperfect human beings, we are, on occasion, selfish, thoughtless, unforgiving, or even cruel. God commands us to behave otherwise. He teaches us to rise above our own imperfections and to treat others with mercy and compassion. When we observe God's Golden Rule, we help build His kingdom here on earth.

The words of Matthew 7:12 remind us that, as believers in Christ, we are commanded to forgive others just as we wish to be forgiven by them. This commandment is, indeed, the Golden Rule for Christians of every generation. When we weave the thread of forgiveness into the very fabric of our lives, we give glory to the One who first forgave us.

A Heart of Forgiveness

Forgiveness is contagious . . . start spreading it around.

The golden rule to follow to obtain spiritual understanding is not one of intellectual pursuit, but one of obedience.

Oswald Chambers

We must mirror God's love in the midst of a world full of hatred. We are the mirrors of God's love, so we may show Jesus by our lives.

Corrie ten Boom

If we have the true love of God in our hearts, we will show it in our lives. We will not have to go up and down the earth proclaiming it. We will show it in everything we say or do.

D. L. Moody

When you extend hospitality to others, you're not trying to impress people, you're trying to reflect God to them.

Max Lucado

Today's Prayer

Dear Lord, let me treat others as I wish to be treated. Because I expect kindness, let me be kind. Because I wish to be loved, let me be loving. Because I need forgiveness, let me be merciful. In all things, Lord, let me live by the Golden Rule, and let me teach that rule to others through my words and my deeds. Amen

Beyond the Complaints

Be hospitable to one another without complaining.

1 Peter 4:9 HCSB

Most of us have more blessings than we can count, yet we can still find reasons to complain about the minor frustrations of everyday life. To do so, of course, is not only shortsighted, but it is also a serious roadblock on the path to spiritual abundance.

Would you like to feel more comfortable about your circumstances and your life? Then promise yourself that you'll do whatever it takes to ensure that you focus your thoughts and energy on the major blessings you've received (not the minor inconveniences you must occasionally endure).

So the next time you're tempted to complain about the inevitable frustrations of everyday living, don't do it! Today and every day, make it a practice to count your blessings, not your hardships. It's the truly decent way to live.

Seeking God's Wisdom

If you're wise, you'll fill your heart with gratitude. When you do, there's simply no room left for complaints.

I am sure it is never sadness—a proper, straight, natural response to loss—that does people harm, but all the other things, all the resentment, dismay, doubt and self-pity with which it is usually complicated.

C. S. Lewis

When you're on the verge of throwing a pity party thanks to your despairing thoughts, go back to the Word of God.

Charles Swindoll

It's your choice: you can either count your blessings or recount your disappointments.

Jim Gallery

He wants us to have a faith that does not complain while waiting, but rejoices because we know our times are in His hands—nail-scarred hands that labor for our highest good.

Kay Arthur

Jesus wept, but he never complained.

C. H. Spurgeon

Today's Prayer

Lord, I know that the choice is mine—I can either count my blessings or recount my disappointments. Today, help me to focus my thoughts upon my blessings, my gifts, and my opportunities. Amen

Be Aware of Your Blessings

Therefore, get your minds ready for action, being self-disciplined, and set your hope completely on the grace to be brought to you at the revelation of Jesus Christ.

1 Peter 1:13 HCSB

Psalm 145 makes this promise: "The LORD is gracious and compassionate, slow to anger and rich in love. The LORD is good to all; he has compassion on all he has made" (vv. 8-9 NIV). As God's children, we are blessed beyond measure, but sometimes, as busy women in a demanding world, we are slow to count our gifts and even slower to give thanks to the Giver. Our blessings include life and health, family and friends, freedom and possessions—for starters. And, the gifts we receive from God are multiplied when we share them with others. May we always give thanks to God for our blessings, and may we always demonstrate our gratitude by sharing them.

Guard Your Heart

God gives us countless blessings. We, in turn, should give Him our thanks and our praise.

Jesus intended for us to be overwhelmed by the blessings of regular days. He said it was the reason he had come: "I am come that they might have life, and that they might have it more abundantly."

Gloria Gaither

Do we not continually pass by blessings innumerable without notice, and instead fix our eyes on what we feel to be our trials and our losses, and think and talk about these until our whole horizon is filled with them, and we almost begin to think we have no blessings at all?

Hannah Whitall Smith

When you and I are related to Jesus Christ, our strength and wisdom and peace and joy and love and hope may run out, but His life rushes in to keep us filled to the brim. We are showered with blessings, not because of anything we have or have not done, but simply because of Him.

Anne Graham Lotz

Today's Prayer

Lord, let me be a woman who counts her blessings, and let me be Your faithful servant as I give praise to the Giver of all things good. You have richly blessed my life, Lord. Let me, in turn, be a blessing to all those who cross my path, and may the glory be Yours forever. Amen

His Disciple

He has told you men what is good and what it is the Lord requires of you: Only to act justly, to love faithfulness, and to walk humbly with your God.

Micah 6:8 HCSB

When Jesus addressed His disciples, He warned that each one must "take up his cross and follow Me." The disciples must have known exactly what the Master meant. In Jesus' day, prisoners were forced to carry their own crosses to the location where they would be put to death. Thus, Christ's message was clear: in order to follow Him, Christ's disciples must deny themselves and, instead, trust Him completely. Nothing has changed since then.

If we are to be disciples of Christ, we must trust Him and place Him at the very center of our beings. Jesus never comes "next." He is always first. The paradox, of course, is that only by sacrificing ourselves to Him do we gain salvation for ourselves.

Do you seek to be a worthy disciple of Christ? Then pick up His cross today and every day that you live. When you do, He will bless you now and forever.

Guard Your Heart

Jesus invites you to become His disciple . . . and the rest is up to you.

Be filled with the Holy Spirit; join a church where the members believe the Bible and know the Lord; seek the fellowship of other Christians; learn and be nourished by God's Word and His many promises. Conversion is not the end of your journey—it is only the beginning.

Corrie ten Boom

When Jesus put the little child in the midst of His disciples, He did not tell the little child to become like His disciples; He told the disciples to become like the little child.

Ruth Bell Graham

Today's Prayer

Dear Lord, thank You for the gift of Your Son Jesus, my personal Savior. Let me be a worthy disciple of Christ, and let me be ever grateful for His love. I offer my life to You, Lord, so that I might live according to Your commandments and according to Your plan. I will praise You always as I give thanks for Your Son and for Your everlasting love. Amen

Wise Choices

As God's slaves, live as free people, but don't use your freedom as a way to conceal evil.

1 Peter 2:16 HCSB

Life is a series of choices. Each day, we make countless decisions that can bring us closer to God…or not. When we live according to God's commandments, we earn for ourselves the abundance and peace that He intends for our lives. But, when we turn our backs upon God by ignoring Him—or by disobeying Him—we bring needless pain and suffering upon ourselves and our families.

Do you want God's peace and His blessings? Then obey Him. When you're faced with a difficult choice or a powerful temptation, seek God's counsel and trust the counsel He gives. Invite God into your heart, accept His forgiveness, and live according to His commandments. And when God speaks to you through that little quiet voice that He has placed in your heart, listen. When you do, you will be blessed today, tomorrow, and forever. And you'll discover that happiness means living in accordance with your beliefs. No exceptions.

A Heart of Forgiveness

God invites you to forgive others. Accept His invitation today.

We have a decision to make—to turn away from sin or to be miserable and suffer the consequences of continual disobedience.

Vonette Bright

Although God causes all things to work together for good for His children, He still holds us accountable for our behavior.

Kay Arthur

There may be no trumpet sound or loud applause when we make a right decision, just a calm sense of resolution and peace.

Gloria Gaither

Today's Prayer

Dear Lord, this world has countless temptations, distractions, interruptions, and frustrations. When I allow my focus to drift away from You and Your Word, I suffer. But, when I turn my thoughts and my prayers to You, Heavenly Father, You guide my path. Let me discover the right thing to do—and let me do it—this day and every day that I live. Amen

Critics Beware

Don't criticize one another, brothers. He who criticizes a brother or judges his brother criticizes the law and judges the law. But if you judge the law, you are not a doer of the law but a judge.

James 4:11 HCSB

From experience, we know that it is easier to criticize than to correct; we understand that it is easier to find faults than solutions; and we realize that excessive criticism is usually destructive, not productive. Yet the urge to criticize others remains a powerful temptation for most of us.

In the book of James, we are issued a clear warning: "Don't criticize one another, brothers" (4:11). Undoubtedly, James understood the paralyzing power of chronic negativity, and so should we.

Negativity is highly contagious: we give it to others who, in turn, give it back to us. This cycle can be broken by positive thoughts, heartfelt prayers, and encouraging words. As thoughtful servants of a loving God, we can use the transforming power of Christ's love to break the chains of negativity. And we should.

A Heart of Forgiveness

If you're too critical of other people—or of yourself—it's time to become more forgiving and less judgmental.

159

When something robs you of your peace of mind, ask yourself if it is worth the energy you are expending on it. If not, then put it out of your mind in an act of discipline. Every time the thought of "it" returns, refuse it.

Kay Arthur

Discouraged people, if they must be discouraged, ought, at least, to keep their discouragements to themselves, hidden away in the privacy of their own bosoms lest they should discourage the hearts of their brethren.

Hannah Whitall Smith

Being critical of others, including God, is one way we try to avoid facing and judging our own sins.

Warren Wiersbe

The scrutiny we give other people should be for ourselves.

Oswald Chambers

Today's Prayer

Help me, Lord, rise above the need to criticize others. May my own shortcomings humble me, and may I always be a source of genuine encouragement to my family and friends. Amen

Focus on the Right Stuff

Let your eyes look forward; fix your gaze straight ahead.

Proverbs 4:25 HCSB

This day—and every day hereafter—is a chance to celebrate the life that God has given you. It's also a chance to give thanks to the One who has offered you more blessings than you can possibly count. What is your focus today? Are you willing to focus your thoughts and energies on God's blessings and upon His will for your life? Or will you turn your thoughts to other things?

Today, why not focus your thoughts on the joy that is rightfully yours in Christ? Why not take time to celebrate God's glorious creation? Why not trust your hopes instead of your fears? When you do, you will think optimistically about yourself and your world . . . and you can then share your optimism with others. They'll be better for it, and so will you. But not necessarily in that order.

Seeking God's Wisdom

When you focus on God's promises, the world's troubles grow increasingly dim.

Measure the size of the obstacles against the size of God.

Beth Moore

We need to stop focusing on our lacks and stop giving out excuses and start looking at and listening to Jesus.

Anne Graham Lotz

What is your focus today? Joy comes when it is Jesus first, others second…then you.

Kay Arthur

Don't let worry rob you of the joy that is rightfully yours. God is in heaven, and He knows your every need. Focus on God and His provisions, and watch gratefully as the worries of today begin to fade away.

Marie T. Freeman

Paul did one thing. Most of us dabble in forty things. Are you a doer or a dabbler?

Vance Havner

Today's Prayer

Dear Lord, help me to face this day with a spirit of optimism and thanksgiving. And let me focus my thoughts on You and Your incomparable gifts. Amen

Consider the Possibilities

But Jesus looked at them and said, "With men this is impossible, but with God all things are possible."

Matthew 19:26 HCSB

All of us face difficult days. Sometimes even the most optimistic women can become discouraged, and you are no exception. If you find yourself enduring difficult circumstances, perhaps it's time for an extreme intellectual makeover—perhaps it's time to focus more on your strengths and opportunities, and less on the challenges that confront you. And one more thing: perhaps it's time to put a little more faith in God.

Every day, including this one, is brimming with possibilities. Every day is filled with opportunities to forgive, to serve, and to share. But if you are entangled in a web of negativity, you may overlook the blessings that God has scattered along your path. So don't give in to pessimism, to doubt, or to cynicism. Instead, keep your eyes upon the possibilities, fix your heart upon the Creator, do your best, and let Him handle the rest.

A Heart of Forgiveness

The road of life contains a number of potholes and stumbling blocks. But, don't invest large quantities of your life focusing on past misfortunes. On the road of life, regret is a dead end.

God specializes in things fresh and firsthand. His plans for you this year may outshine those of the past. He's prepared to fill your days with reasons to give Him praise.

Joni Eareckson Tada

I could go through this day oblivious to the miracles all around me or I could tune in and "enjoy."

Gloria Gaither

When we face an impossible situation, all self-reliance and self-confidence must melt away; we must be totally dependent on Him for the resources.

Anne Graham Lotz

Today's Prayer

Lord, as I take the next steps on my life's journey, let me take them with You. Whatever this day may bring, I thank You for the opportunity to live abundantly. Let me lean upon You, Father—and trust You—this day and forever. Amen

Love According to God

This is My commandment, that you love one another as I have loved you.

John 15:12 NKJV

As a woman, you know the profound love that you hold in your heart for your own family and friends. As a child of God, you can only imagine the infinite love that your Heavenly Father holds for you.

God made you in His own image and gave you salvation through the person of His Son Jesus Christ. And now, precisely because you are a wondrous creation treasured by God, a question presents itself: What will you do in response to the Creator's love? Will you ignore it or embrace it? Will you return it or neglect it? That decision, of course, is yours and yours alone.

When you embrace God's love, your life's purpose is forever changed. When you embrace God's love, you will feel differently about yourself, your neighbors, your family, and your world. More importantly, you will share God's message—and His love—with others.

Your Heavenly Father—a God of infinite love and mercy—is waiting to embrace you with open arms. Accept His love today and forever.

A Heart of Forgiveness

God is love, and He expects you to share His love and His forgiveness with others.

Those who abandon ship the first time it enters a storm miss the calm beyond. And the rougher the storms weathered together, the deeper and stronger real love grows.

Ruth Bell Graham

Love is an attribute of God. To love others is evidence of a genuine faith.

Kay Arthur

Love is the seed of all hope. It is the enticement to trust, to risk, to try, and to go on.

Gloria Gaither

Live your lives in love, the same sort of love which Christ gives us, and which He perfectly expressed when He gave Himself as a sacrifice to God.

Corrie ten Boom

Today's Prayer

Dear Lord, You have given me the gift of love; let me share that gift with others. And, keep me mindful that the essence of love is not to receive it, but to give it, today and forever. Amen

Keep Searching for Wisdom

Now if any of you lacks wisdom, he should ask God, who gives to all generously and without criticizing, and it will be given to him. But let him ask in faith without doubting. For the doubter is like the surging sea, driven and tossed by the wind.

James 1:5-6 HCSB

Where will you find wisdom today? Will you seek it from God or from the world? As a thoughtful woman living in a society that is filled with temptations and distractions, you know that the world's brand of "wisdom" is everywhere . . . and it is dangerous. You live in a world where it's all too easy to stray far from the ultimate source of wisdom: God's Holy Word.

When you commit yourself to the daily study of God's Word—and when you live according to His commandments—you will become wise . . . in time. But don't expect to open your Bible today and be wise tomorrow. Wisdom is not like a mushroom; it does not spring up overnight. It is, instead, like a majestic oak tree that starts as a tiny acorn, grows into a sapling, and eventually reaches up to the sky, tall and strong.

Today and every day, as a way of understanding God's plan for your life, you should study His Word and live by it. When you do, you will accumulate a storehouse of wisdom that will enrich your own life and the lives of your family members, your friends, and the world.

I will instruct you and show you the way to go; with My eye on you, I will give counsel.

Psalm 32:8 HCSB

Wisdom is the principal thing; therefore get wisdom. And in all your getting, get understanding.

Proverbs 4:7 NKJV

Therefore, everyone who hears these words of Mine and acts on them will be like a sensible man who built his house on the rock. The rain fell, the rivers rose, and the winds blew and pounded that house. Yet it didn't collapse, because its foundation was on the rock.

Matthew 7:24-25 HCSB

Seeking God's Wisdom

God makes His wisdom available to you. Your job is to acknowledge, to understand, and (above all) to use that wisdom.

If we neglect the Bible, we cannot expect to benefit from the wisdom and direction that result from knowing God's Word.

Vonette Bright

Knowledge can be found in books or in school. Wisdom, on the other hand, starts with God . . . and ends there.

Marie T. Freeman

Wisdom is knowledge applied. Head knowledge is useless on the battlefield. Knowledge stamped on the heart makes one wise.

Beth Moore

When you and I are related to Jesus Christ, our strength and wisdom and peace and joy and love and hope may run out, but His life rushes in to keep us filled to the brim. We are showered with blessings, not because of anything we have or have not done, but simply because of Him.

Anne Graham Lotz

Today's Prayer

Lord, make me a woman of wisdom and discernment. I seek wisdom, Lord, not as the world gives, but as You give. Lead me in Your ways and teach me from Your Word so that, in time, my wisdom might glorify Your kingdom and Your Son. Amen

Look for Fulfillment in All the Right Places

I am the door. If anyone enters by Me, he will be saved, and will come in and go out and find pasture.

John 10:9 HCSB

Where can you find contentment? Is it a result of wealth, or power, or beauty, or fame? Hardly. Genuine contentment springs from a peaceful spirit, a clear conscience, and a loving heart (like yours!).

Our modern world seems preoccupied with the search for happiness. We are bombarded with messages telling us that happiness depends upon the acquisition of material possessions. These messages are false. Enduring peace is not the result of our acquisitions; it is the inevitable result of our dispositions. If we don't find contentment within ourselves, we will never find it outside ourselves.

Thus the search for contentment is an internal quest, an exploration of the heart, mind, and soul. You can find contentment—indeed you will find it—if you simply look in the right places. And the best time to start looking in those places is now.

Guard Your Heart

God offers you His peace, His protection, and His promises. If you accept these gifts, you will be content.

When we do what is right, we have contentment, peace, and happiness.

Beverly LaHaye

Father and Mother lived on the edge of poverty, and yet their contentment was not dependent upon their surroundings. Their relationship to each other and to the Lord gave them strength and happiness.

Corrie ten Boom

I believe that in every time and place it is within our power to acquiesce in the will of God—and what peace it brings to do so!

Elisabeth Elliot

The key to contentment is to consider. Consider who you are and be satisfied with that. Consider what you have and be satisfied with that. Consider what God's doing and be satisfied with that.

Luci Swindoll

Today's Prayer

Father, let me be a woman who strives to do Your will here on earth, and as I do, let me find contentment and balance. Let me live in the light of Your will and Your priorities for my life, and when I have done my best, Lord, give me the wisdom to place my faith and my trust in You. Amen

Open Up Your Heart

We know that all things work together for the good of those who love God: those who are called according to His purpose.

Romans 8:28 HCSB

C. S. Lewis observed, "A man's spiritual health is exactly proportional to his love for God." If we are to enjoy the spiritual health that God intends for us, we must praise Him, we must love Him, and we must obey Him.

When we worship God faithfully and obediently, we invite His love into our hearts. When we truly worship God, we allow Him to rule over our days and our lives. In turn, we grow to love God even more deeply as we sense His love for us.

St. Augustine wrote, "I love you, Lord, not doubtingly, but with absolute certainty. Your Word beat upon my heart until I fell in love with you, and now the universe and everything in it tells me to love you."

Today, open your heart to the Father. And let your obedience be a fitting response to His never-ending love.

A Heart of Forgiveness

One way that you demonstrate your love to God is by obeying His commandment to forgive others, just as He has forgiven you.

Joy is a by-product not of happy circumstances, education or talent, but of a healthy relationship with God and a determination to love Him no matter what.

Barbara Johnson

Delighting thyself in the Lord is the sudden realization that He has become the desire of your heart.

Beth Moore

Loving Him means the thankful acceptance of all things that His love has appointed.

Elisabeth Elliot

When an honest soul can get still before the living Christ, we can still hear Him say simply and clearly, "Love the Lord your God with all your heart and with all your soul and with all your mind…and love one another as I have loved you."

Gloria Gaither

Today's Prayer

Dear Heavenly Father, You have blessed me with a love that is infinite and eternal. Let me love You, Lord, more and more each day. Make me a loving servant, Father, today and throughout eternity. And, let me show my love for You by sharing Your message and Your love with others. Amen

Be a Cheerful Christian

A cheerful heart has a continual feast.

Proverbs 15:15 HCSB

On some days, as every woman knows, it's hard to be cheerful. Sometimes, as the demands of the world increase and our energy sags, we feel less like "cheering up" and more like "tearing up." But even in our darkest hours, we can turn to God, and He will give us comfort.

Few things in life are more sad, or, for that matter, more absurd, than a grumpy Christian. Christ promises us lives of abundance and joy, but He does not force His joy upon us. We must claim His joy for ourselves, and when we do, Jesus, in turn, fills our spirits with His power and His love.

How can we receive from Christ the joy that is rightfully ours? By giving Him what is rightfully His: our hearts and our souls.

When we earnestly commit ourselves to the Savior of mankind, and when we place Jesus at the center of our lives and trust Him as our personal Savior, He will transform us, not just for today, but for all eternity. Then we, as God's children, can share Christ's joy and His message with a world that needs both.

Guard Your Heart

Cheerfulness is its own reward—but not its only reward.

We may run, walk, stumble, drive, or fly, but let us never lose sight of the reason for the journey, or miss a chance to see a rainbow on the way.

Gloria Gaither

When we bring sunshine into the lives of others, we're warmed by it ourselves. When we spill a little happiness, it splashes on us.

Barbara Johnson

God is good, and heaven is forever. And if those two facts don't cheer you up, nothing will.

Marie T. Freeman

Today's Prayer

Dear Lord, You have given me so many reasons to celebrate. Today, let me choose an attitude of cheerfulness. Let me be a joyful Christian, Lord, quick to smile and slow to anger. And, let me share Your goodness with all whom I meet so that Your love might shine in me and through me. Amen

Trusting God's Will

God is my shield, saving those whose hearts are true and right.

Psalm 7:10 NLT

God has will, and so do we. He gave us the power to make choices for ourselves, and He created a world in which those choices have consequences. The ultimate choice that we face, of course, is what to do about God. We can cast our lot with Him by choosing Jesus Christ as our personal Savior, or not. The choice is ours alone.

We also face thousands of small choices that make up the fabric of daily life. When we align those choices with God's commandments, and when we align our lives with God's will, we receive His abundance, His peace, and His joy. But when we struggle against God's will for our lives, we reap a bitter harvest indeed.

Today, you'll face thousands of small choices; as you do, use God's Word as your guide. And, as you face the ultimate choice, place God's Son and God's will and God's love at the center of your life. You'll discover that God's plan is far grander than any you could have imagined.

Seeking God's Wisdom

When God's will becomes your will, good things happen.

Make God's will the focus of your life day by day. If you seek to please Him and Him alone, you'll find yourself satisfied with life.

Kay Arthur

To yield to God means to belong to God, and to belong to God means to have all His infinite power. To belong to God means to have all.

Hannah Whitall Smith

The will of God is never exactly what you expect it to be. It may seem to be much worse, but in the end it's going to be a lot better and a lot bigger.

Elisabeth Elliot

Jesus yielded Himself to the Father's will. He was a model of "reverent submission." Jesus lived a life of prayer, faith, and obedience.

Shirley Dobson

Today's Prayer

Heavenly Father, in these quiet moments before this busy day unfolds, I come to You. I will study Your Word and seek Your guidance. Give me the wisdom to know Your will for my life and the courage to follow wherever You may lead me, today and forever. Amen

Pray About Your Decisions

Now if any of you lacks wisdom, he should ask God, who gives to all generously and without criticizing, and it will be given to him. But let him ask in faith without doubting. For the doubter is like the surging sea, driven and tossed by the wind.

James 1:5-6 HCSB

Have you fervently asked God for His guidance in every aspect of your life? If so, then you're continually inviting your Creator to reveal Himself in a variety of ways. As a follower of Christ, you must do no less.

Jesus made it clear to His disciples: they should pray always. So should we. Genuine, heartfelt prayer produces powerful changes in us and in our world. When we lift our hearts to our Father in heaven, we open ourselves to a never-ending source of divine wisdom and infinite love.

Do you have questions about your future that you simply can't answer? Ask for the guidance of your Heavenly Father. Do you sincerely seek to know God's purpose for your life? Then ask Him for direction—and keep asking Him every day that you live. Whatever your need, no matter how great or small, pray about it and never lose hope. God is not just near; He is here, and He's ready to talk with you. Now!

A Heart of Forgiveness

Prayer changes things, it changes you, and it changes other people. So pray.

Are you weak? Weary? Confused? Troubled? Pressured? How is your relationship with God? Is it held in its place of priority? I believe the greater the pressure, the greater your need for time alone with Him.

Kay Arthur

When there is a matter that requires definite prayer, pray until you believe God and until you can thank Him for His answer.

Hannah Whitall Smith

A prayerful heart and an obedient heart will learn, very slowly and not without sorrow, to stake everything on God Himself.

Elisabeth Elliot

Today's Prayer

Dear Lord, I will be a woman of prayer. I will pray about matters great and small. I will bring my concerns to You, Father. I will listen for Your voice, and I will follow in the footsteps of Your Son. Amen

He's Right Here, Right Now

The Lord is with you when you are with Him. If you seek Him, He will be found by you.

2 Chronicles 15:2 HCSB

Since God is everywhere, we are free to sense His presence whenever we take the time to quiet our souls and turn our prayers to Him. But sometimes, amid the incessant demands of everyday life, we turn our thoughts far from God; when we do, we suffer.

Do you set aside quiet moments each day to offer praise to your Creator? As a woman who has received the gift of God's grace, you most certainly should. Silence is a gift that you give to yourself and to God. During these moments of stillness, you will often sense the infinite love and power of your Creator—and He, in turn, will speak directly to your heart.

The familiar words of Psalm 46:10 remind us to "Be still, and know that I am God." When we do so, we encounter the awesome presence of our loving Heavenly Father, and we are comforted in the knowledge that God is not just near. He is here.

Guard Your Heart

God isn't far away—He's right here, right now. And He's willing to talk to you right here, right now.

*Draw near to God,
and He will draw near to you.*

—

James 4:8 HCSB

It's a crazy world and life speeds by at a blur, yet God is right in the middle of the craziness. And anywhere, at anytime, we may turn to Him, hear His voice, feel His hand, and catch the fragrance of heaven.

Joni Eareckson Tada

Our souls were made to live in an upper atmosphere, and we stifle and choke if we live on any lower level. Our eyes were made to look off from these heavenly heights, and our vision is distorted by any lower gazing.

Hannah Whitall Smith

Through the death and broken body of Jesus Christ on the Cross, you and I have been given access to the presence of God when we approach Him by faith in prayer.

Anne Graham Lotz

Today's Prayer

Heavenly Father, help me to feel Your presence in every situation and every circumstance. You are with me, Lord, in times of celebration and in times of sorrow. You are with me when I am strong and when I am weak. You never leave my side even when it seems to me that You are far away. Today and every day, God, let me feel You and acknowledge Your presence so that others, too, might know You through me. Amen

Moving Mountains

I assure you: If anyone says to this mountain, "Be lifted up and thrown into the sea," and does not doubt in his heart, but believes that what he says will happen, it will be done for him.

Mark 11:23 HCSB

When a suffering woman sought healing by simply touching the hem of His garment, Jesus turned and said, "Daughter, be of good comfort; thy faith hath made thee whole" (Matthew 9:22 KJV). We, too, can be made whole when we place our faith completely and unwaveringly in the person of Jesus Christ.

Concentration camp survivor Corrie ten Boom relied on faith during her ten months of imprisonment and torture. Later, despite the fact that four of her family members had died in Nazi death camps, Corrie's faith was unshaken. She wrote, "There is no pit so deep that God's love is not deeper still." Christians take note: Genuine faith in God means faith in all circumstances, happy or sad, joyful or tragic.

If your faith is being tested to the point of breaking, know that your Savior is near. If you reach out to Him in faith, He will give you peace and heal your broken spirit. Be content to touch even the smallest fragment of the Master's garment, and He will make you whole.

The Power of Faith

If your faith is strong enough, you and God—working together—can move mountains.

Faith is seeing light with the eyes of your heart, when the eyes of your body see only darkness.

Barbara Johnson

Grace calls you to get up, throw off your blanket of helplessness, and to move on through life in faith.

Kay Arthur

Just as our faith strengthens our prayer life, so do our prayers deepen our faith. Let us pray often, starting today, for a deeper, more powerful faith.

Shirley Dobson

If God chooses to remain silent, faith is content.

Ruth Bell Graham

Today's Prayer

Dear Lord, help me to be a woman of faith. Help me to remember that You are always near and that You can overcome any challenge. With Your love and Your power, Lord, I can live courageously and faithfully today and every day. Amen

Worry Less

Don't worry about anything, but in everything, through prayer and petition with thanksgiving, let your requests be made known to God.

Philippians 4:6 HCSB

If you are like most women, it is simply a fact of life: from time to time, you worry. You worry about health, about finances, about safety, about relationships, about family, and about countless other challenges of life, some great and some small. Where is the best place to take your worries? Take them to God. Take your troubles to Him, and your fears, and your sorrows.

Barbara Johnson correctly observed, "Worry is the senseless process of cluttering up tomorrow's opportunities with leftover problems from today." So if you'd like to make the most out of this day (and every one hereafter), turn your worries over to a Power greater than yourself . . . and spend your valuable time and energy solving the problems you can fix . . . while trusting God to do the rest.

Seeking God's Wisdom

Work hard, pray harder, and if you have any worries, take them to God—and leave them there.

Your heart must not be troubled.
Believe in God; believe also in Me.

—

John 14:1 HCSB

Worry is the senseless process of cluttering up tomorrow's opportunities with leftover problems from today.

Barbara Johnson

We are not called to be burden-bearers, but cross-bearers and light-bearers. We must cast our burdens on the Lord.

Corrie ten Boom

This life of faith, then, consists in just this—being a child in the Father's house. Let the ways of childish confidence and freedom from care, which so please you and win your heart when you observe your own little ones, teach you what you should be in your attitude toward God.

Hannah Whitall Smith

Worries carry responsibilities that belong to God, not to you. Worry does not enable us to escape evil; it makes us unfit to cope with it when it comes.

Corrie ten Boom

Today's Prayer

Dear Lord, wherever I find myself, let me celebrate more and worry less. When my faith begins to waver, help me to trust You more. Then, with praise on my lips and the love of Your Son in my heart, let me live courageously, faithfully, prayerfully, and thankfully this day and every day. Amen

Getting It Done Now

When you make a vow to God, don't delay fulfilling it, because He does not delight in fools. Fulfill what you vow.

Ecclesiastes 5:4 HCSB

The old saying is both familiar and true: actions speak louder than words. And as believers, we must beware: our actions should always give credence to the changes that Christ can make in the lives of those who walk with Him.

God calls upon each of us to act in accordance with His will and with respect for His commandments. If we are to be responsible believers, we must realize that it is never enough simply to hear the instructions of God; we must also live by them. And it is never enough to wait idly by while others do God's work here on earth; we, too, must act. Doing God's work is a responsibility that each of us must bear, and when we do, our loving Heavenly Father rewards our efforts with a bountiful harvest.

A Heart of Forgiveness

Because actions do speak louder than words, it's always a good time to let your actions speak for themselves.

We spend our lives dreaming of the future, not realizing that a little of it slips away every day.

Barbara Johnson

A bird does not know it can fly before it uses its wings. We learn God's love in our hearts as soon as we act upon it.

Corrie ten Boom

From the very moment one feels called to act is born the strength to bear whatever horror one will feel or see. In some inexplicable way, terror loses its overwhelming power when it becomes a task that must be faced.

Emmi Bonhoeffer

God has lots of folks who intend to go to work for him "some day." What He needs is more people who are willing to work for Him this day.

Marie T. Freeman

Today's Prayer

Dear Lord, I have heard Your Word, and I have felt Your presence in my heart; let me act accordingly. Let my words and deeds serve as a testimony to the changes You have made in my life. Let me praise You, Father, by following in the footsteps of Your Son, and let others see Him through me. Amen

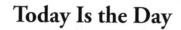

Today Is the Day

We must do the works of Him who sent Me while it is day. Night is coming when no one can work.

John 9:4 HCSB

The words of John 9:4 remind us that "night is coming" for all of us. But until then, God gives us each day and fills it to the brim with possibilities. The day is presented to us fresh and clean at midnight, free of charge, but we must beware: Today is a non-renewable resource—once it's gone, it's gone forever. Our responsibility, of course, is to use this day in the service of God's will and in accordance with His commandments.

Today is a priceless gift that has been given to you by God—don't waste it. Don't stand on the sidelines as life's parade passes you by. Instead, search for the hidden possibilities that God has placed along your path. This day is a one-of-a-kind treasure that can be put to good use—or not. Your challenge is to use this day joyfully and productively. And while you're at it, encourage others to do likewise. After all, night is coming when no one can work . . .

Guard Your Heart

Today is a wonderful, one-of-a-kind gift from God. Treat it that way.

Yesterday is the tomb of time, and tomorrow is the womb of time. Only now is yours.

R. G. Lee

Christ is the secret, the source, the substance, the center, and the circumference of all true and lasting gladness.

Mrs. Charles E. Cowman

If we are ever going to be or do anything for our Lord, now is the time.

Vance Havner

Jesus intended for us to be overwhelmed by the blessings of regular days. He said it was the reason he had come: "I am come that they might have life, and that they might have it more abundantly."

Gloria Gaither

Today's Prayer

This is the day that You have given me, Lord. Let me be thankful, and let me use it according to Your plan. I praise You, Father, for the gift of life and for the friends and family members who make my life rich. Enable me to live each moment to the fullest, totally involved in Your will. Amen

Forgive and Move On

And be kind and compassionate to one another, forgiving one another, just as God also forgave you in Christ.

Ephesians 4:32 HCSB

The old saying is familiar: "Forgive and forget." But when we have been hurt badly, forgiveness is often difficult and forgetting is downright impossible. What, then, are we to do? Even though we cannot forget the past, we must learn to forgive those who have injured us. Forgetting may be unrealistic, but forgiving is not.

Since we can't forget yesterday's troubles, we should learn from them. We should learn from our own mistakes and from the mistakes of others. If we are observant and wise, yesterday has much to teach us about tomorrow. Yet even though we may learn from the past, we should never live in the past. God has given each of us a glorious day: this one. And it's up to each of us to use this day as faithful stewards, not as embittered historians.

So if you're trying to forget the past, don't waste your time. Instead, try a different approach: learn to accept the past and live in the present. Then, you can focus your thoughts and your energies, not on the struggles of yesterday, but instead on the profound opportunities that God has placed before you today.

A Heart of Forgiveness

When you encounter situations that you cannot change, you must learn the wisdom of acceptance . . . and you must learn to trust God.

He is the Lord.
He will do what He thinks is good.

—

1 Samuel 3:18 HCSB

Two words will help you cope when you run low on hope: accept and trust.

Charles Swindoll

It is always possible to do the will of God. In every place and time it is within our power to acquiesce in the will of God.

Elisabeth Elliot

The one true way of dying to self is the way of patience, meekness, humility, and resignation to God.

Andrew Murray

Acceptance says: True, this is my situation at the moment. I'll look unblinkingly at the reality of it. But, I'll also open my hands to accept willingly whatever a loving Father sends me.

Catherine Marshall

Today's Prayer

Dear Lord, let me live in the present, not the past. Let me focus on my blessings, not my sorrows. Give me the wisdom to be thankful for the gifts that I do have, and not bitter about the things that I don't have. Let me accept what was, let me give thanks for what is, and let me have faith in what most surely will be: the promise of eternal life with You. Amen

The Power of Encouragement

Patience and encouragement come from God. And I pray that God will help you all agree with each other the way Christ Jesus wants.

Romans 15:5 NCV

Are you a woman who is a continuing source of encouragement to your family and friends? Hopefully so. After all, one of the reasons that God put you here is to serve and encourage other people—starting with the people who live under your roof.

In his letter to the Ephesians, Paul writes, "Do not let any unwholesome talk come out of your mouths, but only what is helpful for building others up according to their needs, that it may benefit those who listen" (4:29 NIV). This passage reminds us that, as Christians, we are instructed to choose our words carefully so as to build others up through wholesome, honest encouragement. How can we build others up? By celebrating their victories and their accomplishments. As the old saying goes, "When someone does something good, applaud—you'll make two people happy."

Today, look for the good in others and celebrate the good that you find. When you do, you'll be a powerful force of encouragement in your corner of the world . . . and a worthy servant to your God.

Therefore encourage one another and build each other up as you are already doing.

1 Thessalonians 5:11 HCSB

Finally, brothers, rejoice. Be restored, be encouraged, be of the same mind, be at peace, and the God of love and peace will be with you.

2 Corinthians 13:11 HCSB

For this very reason, make every effort to supplement your faith with goodness, goodness with knowledge, knowledge with self-control, self-control with endurance, endurance with godliness.

2 Peter 1:5-6 HCSB

No rotten talk should come from your mouth, but only what is good for the building up of someone in need, in order to give grace to those who hear.

Ephesians 4:29 HCSB

Seeking God's Wisdom

God's Word encourages you to encourage others. Enough said.

Always stay connected to people and seek out things that bring you joy. Dream with abandon. Pray confidently.

Barbara Johnson

A single word, if spoken in a friendly spirit, may be sufficient to turn one from dangerous error.

Fanny Crosby

The glory of friendship is not the outstretched hand, or the kindly smile, or the joy of companionship. It is the spiritual inspiration that comes to one when he discovers that someone else believes in him and is willing to trust him with his friendship.

Corrie ten Boom

One of the ways God refills us after failure is through the blessing of Christian fellowship. Just experiencing the joy of simple activities shared with other children of God can have a healing effect on us.

Anne Graham Lotz

Today's Prayer

Dear Lord, let me celebrate the accomplishments of others. Make me a source of genuine, lasting encouragement to my family and friends. And let my words and deeds be worthy of Your Son, the One who gives me strength and salvation, this day and for all eternity. Amen

Put Faith Above Feelings

Now the just shall live by faith.

Hebrews 10:38 NKJV

Who is in charge of your emotions? Is it you, or have you formed the unfortunate habit of letting other people—or troubling situations—determine the quality of your thoughts and the direction of your day? If you're wise—and if you'd like to build a better life for yourself and your loved ones—you'll learn to control your emotions before your emotions control you.

Human emotions are highly variable, decidedly unpredictable, and often unreliable. Our emotions are like the weather, only far more fickle. So we must learn to live by faith, not by the ups and downs of our own emotional roller coasters.

Sometime, you will probably be gripped by a strong negative feeling. Distrust it. Reign it in. Test it. And turn it over to God. Your emotions will inevitably change; God will not. So trust Him completely as you watch those negative feelings slowly evaporate into thin air.

Seeking God's Wisdom

Here are the facts: God's love is real; His peace is real; His support is real. Don't ever let your emotions obscure these facts.

Emotions we have not poured out in the safe hands of God can turn into feelings of hopelessness and depression. God is safe.

Beth Moore

The only serious mistake we can make is the mistake that Psalm 121 prevents: the mistake of supposing that God's interest in us waxes and wanes in response to our spiritual temperature.

Eugene Peterson

Before you can dry another's tears, you too must weep.

Barbara Johnson

Don't bother much about your feelings. When they are humble, loving, brave, give thanks for them; when they are conceited, selfish, cowardly, ask to have them altered. In neither case are they you, but only a thing that happens to you. What matters is your intentions and your behavior.

C. S. Lewis

Today's Prayer

Heavenly Father, You are my strength and my refuge. As I journey through this day, I will encounter events that cause me emotional distress. Lord, when I am troubled, let me turn to You. Keep me steady, Lord, and in those difficult moments, renew a right spirit inside my heart. Amen

God Forgives Us and We Must Forgive Others

And whenever you stand praying, if you have anything against anyone, forgive him, so that your Father in heaven may also forgive you your wrongdoing.

Mark 11:25 HCSB

God's power to forgive, like His love, is infinite. Despite your shortcomings, despite your sins, God offers you immediate forgiveness and eternal life when you accept Christ as your Savior.

As a believer who is the recipient of God's forgiveness, how should you behave towards others? Should you forgive them (just as God has forgiven you), or should you remain embittered and resentful? The answer, of course, is found in God's Word: you are instructed to forgive others. When you do, you not only obey God's command, you also free yourself from a prison of your own making.

When it comes to forgiveness, God doesn't play favorites and neither should you. You should forgive all those who have harmed you (not just the people who have asked for forgiveness or those who have made restitution). Complete forgiveness is God's way, and it should be your way, too. Anything less is an affront to Him and a burden to you.

Guard Your Heart

When all else fails, God's love does not. You can always depend upon God's love . . . and He is always your ultimate protection.

Snuggle in God's arms. When you are hurting, when you feel lonely or left out, let Him cradle you, comfort you, reassure you of His all-sufficient power and love.

Kay Arthur

Being loved by Him whose opinion matters most gives us the security to risk loving, too—even loving ourselves.

Gloria Gaither

There is no pit so deep that God's love is not deeper still.

Corrie ten Boom

Today's Prayer

Dear God, You are love. You love me, Father, and I love You. As I love You more, Lord, I am also able to love my family and friends more. I will be Your loving servant, Heavenly Father, today and throughout eternity. Amen

Choosing to Stand Up for Your Beliefs

You love Him, though you have not seen Him. And though not seeing Him now, you believe in Him and rejoice with inexpressible and glorious joy, because you are receiving the goal of your faith, the salvation of your souls.

1 Peter 1:8-9 HCSB

We must do our best to make sure that our actions are accurate reflections of our beliefs. Our theology must be demonstrated, not only by our words but, more importantly, by our actions. In short, we should be practical women, quick to act upon the beliefs that we hold most dear.

We may proclaim our beliefs to our hearts' content, but our proclamations will mean nothing—to others or to ourselves—unless we accompany our words with deeds that match. The sermons that we live are far more compelling than the ones we preach.

Like it or not, your life is an accurate reflection of your creed. If this fact gives you cause for concern, don't bother talking about the changes that you intend to make—make them. Now.

Guard Your Heart

When you live in sync with your beliefs, God will guide your steps and protect your heart.

Jesus taught that the evidence that confirms our leaps of faith comes after we risk believing, not before.

Gloria Gaither

Faith sees the invisible, believes the unbelievable, and receives the impossible.

Corrie ten Boom

Every man must do two things alone; he must do his own believing and his own dying.

Martin Luther

Faith is not a feeling; it is action. It is a willed choice.

Elisabeth Elliot

Today's Prayer

Heavenly Father, I believe in You, and I believe in Your Word. Help me to live in such a way that my actions validate my beliefs—and let the glory be Yours forever. Amen

Keep Praying and Keep Growing

Like newborn infants, desire the unadulterated spiritual milk, so that you may grow by it in your salvation.

1 Peter 2:2 HCSB

Forgiveness is an exercise in spiritual growth: the more we forgive, the more we grow. Conversely, bitterness makes spiritual growth impossible: when our hearts are filled with resentment and anger, there is no room left for love.

When we cease to grow, either emotionally or spiritually, we do ourselves and our loved ones a profound disservice. But, if we continue to study, pray, and obey, and if we live in the center of His will, we will not be stagnant. We will, instead, continue to grow.

In those quiet moments when we open our hearts to God, the Creator who made us keeps remaking us. He gives us direction, perspective, and wisdom—and He gives us the courage to forgive other folks sooner rather than later, which, by the way, is exactly what we should do.

A Heart of Forgiveness

One way to guard your heart is by continuing to grow in your faith.

*For this reason we also, since the day
we heard it, do not cease to pray for you,
and to ask that you may be filled
with the knowledge of
His will in all wisdom and spiritual
understanding.*

—

Colossians 1:9 NKJV

If you want to discover your spiritual gifts, start obeying God. As you serve Him, you will find that He has given you the gifts that are necessary to follow through in obedience.

Anne Graham Lotz

We set our eyes on the finish line, forgetting the past, and straining toward the mark of spiritual maturity and fruitfulness.

Vonette Bright

A spiritual gift is a manifestation of God at work through you. God works in and through you to bear fruit. The focus is on God and what He does through you.

Henry Blackaby and Claude King

You are either becoming more like Christ every day or you're becoming less like Him. There is no neutral position in the Lord.

Stormie Omartian

Today's Prayer

Dear Lord, thank You for the opportunity to walk with Your Son. And, thank You for the opportunity to grow closer to You each day. I thank You for the person I am . . . and for the person I can become. Amen

Experiencing Silence

Be still, and know that I am God.

Psalm 46:10 NKJV

The world seems to grow louder day by day, and our senses seem to be invaded at every turn. If we allow the distractions of a clamorous society to separate us from God's peace, we do ourselves a profound disservice. Our task, as dutiful believers, is to carve out moments of silence in a world filled with noise.

If we are to maintain righteous minds and compassionate hearts, we must take time each day for prayer and for meditation. We must make ourselves still in the presence of our Creator. We must quiet our minds and our hearts so that we might sense God's will and His love.

Has the busy pace of life robbed you of the peace that God has promised? If so, it's time to reorder your priorities and your life. Nothing is more important than the time you spend with your Heavenly Father. So be still and claim the inner peace that is found in the silent moments you spend with God.

Guard Your Heart

Spend a few moments each day in silence. You owe it to your Creator . . . and to yourself.

*Be silent before the Lord and wait
expectantly for Him.*

—

Psalm 37:7 HCSB

Because Jesus Christ is our Great High Priest, not only can we approach God without a human "go-between," we can also hear and learn from God in some sacred moments without one.

Beth Moore

In the soul-searching of our lives, we are to stay quiet so we can hear Him say all that He wants to say to us in our hearts.

Charles Swindoll

It is in that stillness that the Voice will be heard, the only voice in all the universe that speaks peace to the deepest part of us.

Elisabeth Elliot

Instead of waiting for the feeling, wait upon God. You can do this by growing still and quiet, then expressing in prayer what your mind knows is true about Him, even if your heart doesn't feel it at this moment.

Shirley Dobson

Today's Prayer

Dear Lord, help me remember the importance of silence. Help me discover quiet moments throughout the day so that I can sense Your presence and Your love. Amen

God's Timetable

He has made everything appropriate in its time. He has also put eternity in their hearts, but man cannot discover the work God has done from beginning to end.

Ecclesiastes 3:11 HCSB

I f you sincerely seek to be a woman of faith, then you must learn to trust God's timing. You will be sorely tempted, however, to do otherwise. Because you are a fallible human being, you are impatient for things to happen. But, God knows better.

God has created a world that unfolds according to His own timetable, not ours . . . thank goodness! We mortals might make a terrible mess of things. God does not.

God's plan does not always happen in the way that we would like or at the time of our own choosing. Our task—as believing Christians who trust in a benevolent, all-knowing Father—is to wait patiently for God to reveal Himself. And reveal Himself He will. Always. But until God's perfect plan is made known, we must walk in faith and never lose hope. And we must continue to trust Him. Always.

Seeking God's Wisdom

You don't know precisely what you need—or when you need it—but God does. So trust His timing.

*Therefore humble yourselves
under the mighty hand of God,
that He may exalt you in due time.*

—

1 Peter 5:6 NKJV

By his wisdom, he orders his delays so that they prove to be far better than our hurries.

C. H. Spurgeon

When we read of the great Biblical leaders, we see that it was not uncommon for God to ask them to wait, not just a day or two, but for years, until God was ready for them to act.

Gloria Gaither

Waiting on God brings us to the journey's end quicker than our feet.

Mrs. Charles E. Cowman

God's silence is in no way indicative of His activity or involvement in our lives. He may be silent, but He is not still.

Charles Swindoll

Today's Prayer

Dear Lord, Your timing is seldom my timing, but Your timing is always right for me. You are my Father, and You have a plan for my life that is grander than I can imagine. When I am impatient, remind me that You are never early or late. You are always on time, Lord, so let me trust in You . . . always. Amen

Choosing to Let God Transform Your Life

Your old life is dead. Your new life, which is your real life—even though invisible to spectators—is with Christ in God. He is your life.

Colossians 3:3 MSG

Think, for a moment, about the "old" you, the person you were before you invited Christ to reign over your heart. Now, think about the "new" you, the person you have become since then. Is there a difference between the old you and the "new and improved" version? There should be! And that difference should be noticeable not only to you but also to others.

The Bible clearly teaches that when we welcome Christ into our hearts, we become new creations through Him. Our challenge, of course, is to behave ourselves like new creations. When we do, God fills our hearts, He blesses our endeavors, and transforms our lives . . . forever.

A Heart of Forgiveness

Unless you're a more forgiving person because of your relationship with Jesus, your faith isn't what it could be . . . or should be.

If you are God's child,
you are no longer bound to
your past or to what you were.
You are a brand new creature
in Christ Jesus.

—

Kay Arthur

There is so much Heaven around us now if we have eyes for it, because eternity starts when we give ourselves to God.

Gloria Gaither

Conversion is not a blind leap into the darkness. It is a joyous leap into the light that is the love of God.

Corrie ten Boom

Repentance involves a radical change of heart and mind in which we agree with God's evaluation of our sin and then take specific action to align ourselves with His will.

Henry Blackaby

If we accept His invitation to salvation, we live with Him forever. However, if we do not accept because we refuse His only Son as our Savior, then we exclude ourselves from My Father's House. It's our choice.

Anne Graham Lotz

Today's Prayer

Lord, when I accepted Jesus as my personal Savior, You changed me forever and made me whole. Let me share Your Son's message with my friends, with my family, and with the world. You are a God of love, redemption, conversion, and salvation. I will praise You today and forever. Amen

Beyond Fear

But Jesus quickly spoke to them, "Have courage! It is I. Do not be afraid."

Matthew 14:27 NCV

A terrible storm rose quickly on the Sea of Galilee, and the disciples were afraid. Although they had witnessed many miracles, the disciples feared for their lives, so they turned to Jesus, and He calmed the waters and the wind.

Sometimes, we, like Jesus' disciples, feel threatened by the storms of life. When we are fearful, we, too, should turn to Him for comfort and for courage.

The next time you find yourself facing a fear-provoking situation, remember that the One who calmed the wind and the waves is also your personal Savior. Then ask yourself which is stronger: your faith or your fear. The answer should be obvious. So, when the storm clouds form overhead and you find yourself being tossed on the stormy seas of life, remember this: Wherever you are, God is there, too. And, because He cares for you, you are protected.

A Heart of Forgiveness

If you're feeling angry or anxious, you must trust God to solve the problems that are simply too big for you to solve.

If a person fears God, he or she has no reason to fear anything else. On the other hand, if a person does not fear God, then fear becomes a way of life.

Beth Moore

Worry is a cycle of inefficient thoughts whirling around a center of fear.

Corrie ten Boom

God shields us from most of the things we fear, but when He chooses not to shield us, He unfailingly allots grace in the measure needed.

Elisabeth Elliot

Fear and doubt are conquered by a faith that rejoices. And faith can rejoice because the promises of God are as certain as God Himself.

Kay Arthur

Today's Prayer

Dear Lord, when I am fearful, keep me mindful that You are my protector and my salvation. Thank You, Father, for a perfect love that casts out fear. Because of You, I can live courageously and faithfully this day and every day. Amen

New Beginnings

Then the One seated on the throne said, "Look! I am making everything new."

Revelation 21:5 HCSB

Each new day offers countless opportunities to serve God, to seek His will, and to obey His teachings. But each day also offers countless opportunities to stray from God's commandments and to wander far from His path.

Sometimes, we wander aimlessly in a wilderness of our own making, but God has better plans for us. And, whenever we ask Him to renew our strength and guide our steps, He does so.

Consider this day a new beginning. Consider it a fresh start, a renewed opportunity to serve your Creator with willing hands and a loving heart. Ask God to renew your sense of purpose as He guides your steps. Today is a glorious opportunity to forgive others and to serve God. Seize those opportunities while you can; tomorrow may indeed be too late.

Seeking God's Wisdom

If you're graduating into a new phase of life, be sure to make God your partner. If you do, He'll guide your steps, He'll help carry your burdens, and He'll help you focus on the things that really matter.

God is not running an antique shop! He is making all things new!

Vance Havner

The amazing thing about Jesus is that He doesn't just patch up our lives, He gives us a brand new sheet, a clean slate to start over, all new.

Gloria Gaither

Like a spring of pure water, God's peace in our hearts brings cleansing and refreshment to our minds and bodies.

Billy Graham

Today's Prayer

Dear God, conform me to Your image. Create in me a new heart—a heart that reflects the love that You lavish upon me. When I need to change, Lord, change me, and make me new again. Amen

Tackling Tough Times

God is our refuge and strength, a very present help in trouble.

Psalm 46:1 NKJV

Women of every generation have experienced adversity, and this generation is no different. But, today's women face challenges that previous generations could have scarcely imagined. Thankfully, although the world continues to change, God's love remains constant. And, He remains ready to comfort us and strengthen us whenever we turn to Him.

Psalm 147 promises, "He heals the brokenhearted, and binds their wounds" (v. 3). When we are troubled, we must call upon God, and, in His own time and according to His own plan, He will heal us.

If you are like most women, it is simply a fact of life: from time to time, you worry. You worry about health, about finances, about safety, about relationships, about family, and about countless other challenges of life, some great and some small. Where is the best place to take your worries? Take them to God. Take your troubles to Him, and your fears, and your sorrows. Seek protection from the One who cannot be moved.

We also rejoice in our afflictions, because we know that affliction produces endurance, endurance produces proven character, and proven character produces hope.

Romans 5:3-4 HCSB

The Lord is a refuge for the oppressed, a refuge in times of trouble.

Psalm 9:9 HCSB

For You delivered me from death, even my feet from stumbling, to walk before God in the light of life.

Psalm 56:13 HCSB

Be anxious for nothing, but in everything by prayer and supplication, with thanksgiving, let your requests be made known to God.

Philippians 4:6 NKJV

Guard Your Heart

When times are tough, you should guard your heart by turning it over to God.

We all go through pain and sorrow, but the presence of God, like a warm, comforting blanket, can shield us and protect us, and allow the deep inner joy to surface, even in the most devastating circumstances.

Barbara Johnson

Often the trials we mourn are really gateways into the good things we long for.

Hannah Whitall Smith

If God sends us on stony paths, he provides strong shoes.

Corrie ten Boom

Often God shuts a door in our face so that he can open the door through which he wants us to go.

Catherine Marshall

Today's Prayer

Dear Heavenly Father, when I am troubled, You heal me. When I am afraid, You protect me. When I am discouraged, You lift me up. You are my unending source of strength, Lord; let me turn to You when I am weak. In times of adversity, let me trust Your plan and Your will for my life. And whatever my circumstances, Lord, let me always give the thanks and the glory to You. Amen

Pray Early and Often

Rejoice always! Pray constantly. Give thanks in everything, for this is God's will for you in Christ Jesus.

1 Thessalonians 5:16-18 HCSB

Jesus made it clear to His disciples: they should pray always. And so should we. Genuine, heartfelt prayer changes things and it changes us. When we lift our hearts to our Father in heaven, we open ourselves to a never-ending source of divine wisdom and infinite love.

Have you been unable to forgive someone? Talk to God about it. Do you have questions that you simply can't answer? Ask for the guidance of your Father in heaven. Have you been unable to forgive yourself for something you did long ago? God has forgiven you; now it's your turn to forgive yourself. Do you sincerely seek the gift of peace and wholeness that only God can give? Then obey His commandments and accept the grace of His only begotten Son.

Whatever your need, no matter how great or small, pray about it. Instead of waiting for mealtimes or bedtimes, follow the instruction of your Savior: pray always and never lose heart. And remember: God is not just near; He is here, and He's ready to talk with you. Now.

Guard Your Heart

There's no corner of your life that's too unimportant to pray about, so pray about everything.

What God gives in answer to our prayers will always be the thing we most urgently need, and it will always be sufficient.

Elisabeth Elliot

Your family and friends need your prayers and you need theirs. And God wants to hear those prayers. So what are you waiting for?

Marie T. Freeman

God says we don't need to be anxious about anything; we just need to pray about everything.

Stormie Omartian

When the Holy Spirit comes to dwell within us, I believe we gain a built-in inclination to take our concerns and needs to the Lord in prayer.

Shirley Dobson

Today's Prayer

Lord, I will be a woman of prayer. I will take everything to You in prayer, and when I do, I will trust Your answers. Amen

Obedience Now

Not everyone who says to Me, "Lord, Lord!" will enter the kingdom of heaven, but the one who does the will of My Father in heaven.

Matthew 7:21 HCSB

God's laws are eternal and unchanging: obedience leads to abundance and joy; disobedience leads to disaster. God has given us a guidebook for righteous living called the Holy Bible. If we trust God's Word and live by it, we are blessed.

If you simply can't find it in your heart to forgive someone, perhaps it's time to talk things over with a person you trust. Perhaps that person is a friend or family member. Or perhaps that person is your pastor or your pastoral counselor.

Sometimes, it takes other people to help us see the obvious: forgiveness is a gift that we give to ourselves. It is only when we forgive others that we gain peace for ourselves. It is only when we empty our hearts of bitterness that we can fill our hearts with joy. It is only when we no longer wish unhappiness for others that we can find lasting happiness for ourselves.

If your heart is burdened with anger or regret, talk about it but don't obsess about it. Your goal should be simple: to forgive and move on. Why? Because the person who hurt you may need your forgiveness, but the one who benefits most from your forgiveness is you.

Seeking God's Wisdom

When you are obedient to God, you are secure; when you are not, you are not.

Now he who keeps His commandments abides in Him, and He in him. And by this we know that He abides in us, by the Spirit whom He has given us.

1 John 3:24 NKJV

You shall walk after the Lord your God and fear Him, and keep His commandments and obey His voice, and you shall serve Him and hold fast to Him.

Deuteronomy 13:4 NKJV

When all has been heard, the conclusion of the matter is: fear God and keep His commands.

Ecclesiastes 12:13 HCSB

If they serve Him obediently, they will end their days in prosperity and their years in happiness.

Job 36:11 HCSB

Let us never suppose that obedience is impossible or that holiness is meant only for a select few. Our Shepherd leads us in paths of righteousness—not for our name's sake but for His.

Elisabeth Elliot

I don't always like His decisions, but when I choose to obey Him, the act of obedience still "counts" with Him even if I'm not thrilled about it.

Beth Moore

The cross that Jesus commands you and me to carry is the cross of submissive obedience to the will of God, even when His will includes suffering and hardship and things we don't want to do.

Anne Graham Lotz

You may not always see immediate results, but all God wants is your obedience and faithfulness.

Vonette Bright

Today's Prayer

Dear Lord, make me a woman who is obedient to Your Word. Let me live according to Your commandments. Direct my path far from the temptations and distractions of this world. And, let me discover Your will and follow it, Lord, this day and always. Amen

Find the Courage to Follow God

Be strong and courageous, and do the work. Don't be afraid or discouraged, for the Lord God, my God, is with you. He won't leave you or forsake you.

1 Chronicles 28:20 HCSB

Life can be difficult and discouraging at times. During our darkest moments, God offers us strength and courage if we turn our hearts and our prayers to Him.

As believing Christians, we have every reason to live courageously. After all, the ultimate battle has already been fought and won on the cross at Calvary. But sometimes, because we are imperfect human beings who possess imperfect faith, we fall prey to fear and doubt. The answer to our fears, of course, is God.

The next time you find your courage tested to the limit, remember that God is as near as your next breath. He is your shield and your strength; He is your protector and your deliverer. Call upon Him in your hour of need and then be comforted. Whatever your challenge, whatever your trouble, God can handle it . . . and will!

Seeking God's Wisdom

If you trust God completely and without reservation, you have every reason on earth—and in heaven—to live courageously. And that's precisely what you should do.

Just as courage is faith in good, so discouragement is faith in evil, and, while courage opens the door to good, discouragement opens it to evil.

Hannah Whitall Smith

What is courage? It is the ability to be strong in trust, in conviction, in obedience. To be courageous is to step out in faith—to trust and obey, no matter what.

Kay Arthur

If a person fears God, he or she has no reason to fear anything else. On the other hand, if a person does not fear God, then fear becomes a way of life.

Beth Moore

Today's Prayer

Dear Lord, fill me with Your Spirit and help me face my challenges with courage and determination. Keep me mindful, Father, that You are with me always—and with You by my side, I have nothing to fear. Amen

Sharing Your Faith

But sanctify the Lord God in your hearts, and always be ready to give a defense to everyone who asks you a reason for the hope that is in you.

1 Peter 3:15 HCSB

Our personal testimonies are extremely important, but sometimes, because of shyness or insecurities, we're afraid to share our experiences. And that's unfortunate.

In his second letter to Timothy, Paul shares a message to believers of every generation when he writes, "God has not given us a spirit of timidity" (1:7). Paul's meaning is clear: When sharing our beliefs, we, as Christians, must be courageous, forthright, and unashamed.

We live in a world that desperately needs the healing message of Christ Jesus. Every believer, each in his or her own way, bears responsibility for sharing the Good News of our Savior.

Billy Graham observed, "Our faith grows by expression. If we want to keep our faith, we must share it." If you are a follower of Christ, the time to express your belief in Him is now. You know how He has touched your heart; help Him do the same for others.

Sharing the Good News

Whether you realize it or not, you have a profound responsibility to tell as many people as you can about the eternal life that Christ offers to those who believe in Him.

There are many timid souls whom we jostle morning and evening as we pass them by; but if only the kind word were spoken they might become fully persuaded.

Fanny Crosby

Your light is the truth of the Gospel message itself as well as your witness as to Who Jesus is and what He has done for you. Don't hide it.

Anne Graham Lotz

Choose Jesus Christ! Deny yourself, take up the Cross, and follow Him—for the world must be shown. The world must see, in us, a discernible, visible, startling difference.

Elisabeth Elliot

Today's Prayer

Dear Lord, the life that I live and the words that I speak bear testimony to my faith. Make me a faithful servant of Your Son, and let my testimony be worthy of You. Let my words be sure and true, Lord, and let my actions point others to You. Amen

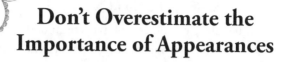

Don't Overestimate the Importance of Appearances

Man does not see what the Lord sees, for man sees what is visible, but the Lord sees the heart.

1 Samuel 16:7 HCSB

Are you worried about keeping up appearances? And as a result, do you spend too much time, energy, or money on things that are intended to make you look good? If so, you are certainly not alone. Ours is a society that focuses intently upon appearances. We are told time and again that we can't be "too thin or too rich." But in truth, the important things in life have little to do with food, fashion, fame, or fortune.

Today, spend less time trying to please the world and more time trying to please your earthly family and your Father in heaven. Focus on pleasing your God and your loved ones, and don't worry too much about trying to impress the folks you happen to pass on the street. It takes too much energy—and too much life—to keep up appearances. So don't waste your energy or your life.

Seeking God's Wisdom

How you appear to other people doesn't make much difference, but how you appear to God makes all the difference.

Outside appearances, things like the clothes you wear or the car you drive, are important to other people but totally unimportant to God. Trust God.

Marie T. Freeman

If the narrative of the Scriptures teaches us anything, from the serpent in the Garden to the carpenter in Nazareth, it teaches us that things are rarely what they seem, that we shouldn't be fooled by appearances.

John Eldredge

It is comfortable to know that we are responsible to God and not to man. It is a small matter to be judged of man's judgement.

Lottie Moon

Comparison is the root of all feelings of inferiority.

James Dobson

Fashion is an enduring testimony to the fact that we live quite consciously before the eyes of others.

John Eldredge

Today's Prayer

Dear Lord, the world sees only my outside appearance, but You see my heart. Today, I will focus, not on outward appearances, but on the reality of our eternal love for me. Amen

Live on Purpose

I, therefore, the prisoner in the Lord, urge you to walk worthy of the calling you have received.

Ephesians 4:1 HCSB

"What on earth does God intend for me to do with my life?" It's an easy question to ask but, for many of us, a difficult question to answer. Why? Because God's purposes aren't always clear to us. Sometimes we wander aimlessly in a wilderness of our own making. And sometimes, we struggle mightily against God in an unsuccessful attempt to find success and happiness through our own means, not His.

If you're a woman who sincerely seeks God's guidance, He will give it. But, He will make His revelations known to you in a way and in a time of His choosing, not yours, so be patient. If you prayerfully petition God and work diligently to discern His intentions, He will, in time, lead you to a place of joyful abundance and eternal peace.

Sometimes, God's intentions will be clear to you; other times, God's plan will seem uncertain at best. But even on those difficult days when you are unsure which way to turn, you must never lose sight of these overriding facts: God created you for a reason; He has important work for you to do; and He's waiting patiently for you to do it.

And the next step is up to you.

Seeking God's Wisdom

God has a plan for your life, a definite purpose that you can fulfill . . . or not. Your challenge is to pray for God's guidance and to follow wherever He leads.

His life is our light—our purpose and meaning and reason for living.

Anne Graham Lotz

Yesterday is just experience but tomorrow is glistening with purpose—and today is the channel leading from one to the other.

Barbara Johnson

Only God's chosen task for you will ultimately satisfy. Do not wait until it is too late to realize the privilege of serving Him in His chosen position for you.

Beth Moore

Today's Prayer

Dear Lord, I know that You have a purpose for my life, and I will seek that purpose today and every day that I live. Let my actions be pleasing to You, and let me share Your Good News with a world that so desperately needs Your healing hand and the salvation of Your Son. Amen

The Ultimate Choice

For God so loved the world that He gave His only begotten Son, that whoever believes in Him should not perish but have everlasting life.

John 3:16 NKJV

Eternal life is not an event that begins when you die. Eternal life begins when you invite Jesus into your heart right here on earth. So it's important to remember that God's plans for you are not limited to the ups and downs of everyday life. If you've allowed Jesus to reign over your heart, you've already begun your eternal journey.

As mere mortals, our vision for the future, like our lives here on earth, is limited. God's vision is not burdened by such limitations: His plans extend throughout all eternity.

Let us praise the Creator for His priceless gift, and let us share the Good News with all who cross our paths. We return our Father's love by accepting His grace and by sharing His message and His love. When we do, we are blessed here on earth and throughout all eternity.

Guard Your Heart

God offers you life abundant and life eternal. Accept His gift today.

And this is the will of Him who sent Me, that everyone who sees the Son and believes in Him may have everlasting life; and I will raise him up at the last day.

—

John 6:40 NKJV

Your choice to either receive
or reject the Lord Jesus Christ
will determine where
you spend eternity.

—

Anne Graham Lotz

I can still hardly believe it. I, with shriveled, bent fingers, atrophied muscles, gnarled knees, and no feeling from the shoulders down, will one day have a new body—light, bright and clothed in righteousness—powerful and dazzling.

Joni Eareckson Tada

God has promised us abundance, peace, and eternal life. These treasures are ours for the asking; all we must do is claim them. One of the great mysteries of life is why on earth do so many of us wait so very long to lay claim to God's gifts?

Marie T. Freeman

Like a shadow declining swiftly...away...like the dew of the morning gone with the heat of the day; like the wind in the treetops, like a wave of the sea, so are our lives on earth when seen in light of eternity.

Ruth Bell Graham

Today's Prayer

I know, Lord, that this world is not my home; I am only here for a brief while. And, You have given me the priceless gift of eternal life through Your Son Jesus. Keep the hope of heaven fresh in my heart, and, while I am in this world, help me to pass through it with faith in my heart and praise on my lips . . . for You. Amen

Judge not, and you shall not be judged.
Condemn not, and
you shall not be condemned.
Forgive, and you will be forgiven.

—

Luke 6:37 NKJV